PICTURESQUE, TECTONIC, ROMANTIC

House Design

HELLIWELL + SMITH

Blue Sky Architecture

PICTURESQUE, TECTONIC, ROMANTIC

House Design
HELLIWELL + SMITH
Blue Sky Architecture

Kim Smith

Bo Helliwell

7

TEXT BY TREVOR BODDY   PREFACE BY PETER DAVEY

First published in Australia in 1999 by
The Images Publishing Group Pty Ltd
ACN 059 734 431
6 Bastow Place, Mulgrave, Victoria 3170, Australia
Telephone: +(61 3) 9561 5544 Facsimile: +(61 3) 9561 4860
E-mail: books@images.com.au

National Library of Australia Cataloguing-in-Publication Data

Picturesque, tectonic, romantic : Helliwell + Smith,
Blue Sky Architecture.

Bibliography.
Includes index.

ISBN 1 86470 028 9.

1. Helliwell, Bo. 2. Smith, Kim, 1953–. 3. Architects.
4. Architecture, Modern – 20th century – Designs and plans.
5. Architecture, Domestic – Designs and plans.
I. Boddy, Trevor, 1953–. (Series : House design; 7).

720.92

Designed by The Graphic Image Studio Pty Ltd
Mulgrave, Australia

Film separations by PageSet Pty. Ltd.

Printed in Hong Kong

PREFACE

by Peter Davey

Blue Sky was born out of the ferment of the late 60s and early 70s, but it has proved to have much more staying power, talent and guts than most other idealistic initiatives of the time. And more bottom. It was not just a northern outpost of the Californian wood-butchers, with which it seemed at first to have so much in common. Blue Sky has always operated on a more sophisticated level than the rather self-absorbed nature-worshipping obsessions of the 'butchers'. Other resonance's are with the thinking of Ruskin, Morris and the Arts and Crafts Movement, with the best of mid-20th century West Coast Modernism and with the tradition of understanding traditional Japanese architecture on the North American side of the Pacific that is much more profound than European japonaiserie (however pretty and entrancing a lot of that may be).

From the first, Bo Helliwell and his colleagues have been regionalists in the best sense of the term. They have been deeply involved with the ecology and topography of southern British Columbia and its wonderful interweave of sea, forest, and rock. But at the same time, they have always been open to ideas and influences from the rest of the world, translating and adapting them to their area, so making architecture that is far more than provincial.

Hornby Island, where most of the early work is to be found, was an unorthodox, inventive place, a haunt of artists and intellectuals: the baker was a sociology professor, and the electrician taught philosophy before deciding to adopt his new trade while writing on the essence of botany. Houses (and ideas) were largely built communally. Architects worked with their hands on site, often generating the buildings without drawings, but only after extensive consultation with the owners before and during construction. Local materials: stone, driftwood, shingles and lumber were used as much as possible. Passive solar design was there from the first. Sometimes early versions of active

12 midnight, Halloween 1997, Peter Davey, Bo Helliwell and Kim Smith

systems were incorporated. Each building was created by designers, users and builders with deep respect for site: for its relief, geology and vegetation, as well as for long prospects over wild nature, and for aspects of the place from afar.

Now, the practice (as carried on by Bo Helliwell and Kim Smith) is rather different, more conventional perhaps, in that it largely works for individual clients and operates from the mainland of West Vancouver, rather than the Island. But the principles imbibed at Hornby continue: ecological consciousness; deep respect for site and user program; craftsmanly involvement with process to generate buildings that are constructively coherent both tectonically and intellectually. Structural geometry has become more sophisticated with experience—think for instance of the Greenwood House on Galiano Island where the building flexes in both plan and section to produce an organic form, which is in the end derived from the site itself.

Blue Sky was not as subtle and nor even as topographically sensitive in the earliest years. Parallel to development of structural sophistication has been refinement of understanding of materiality (perhaps because the new generation of clients can afford rather more than the early ones). For instance, in the Greenwood House, floor finishes are chosen with great care: warm cherry-wood unites all the main living areas; hard-wearing stone flags are under the kitchen area; and where inevitably your naked feet make contact with the floor, in the shower, the surface is made of thin sea-smoothed pebbles, laid on edge to provide a gently corrugated and comforting surface. The cherry-wood is a rather exotic addition to a palette of materials that has always been concerned with appealing to all the senses: hearing, touch, scent as well as sight, in which dimension wood has always warmed the often dull grey light of British Columbia as it penetrates the buildings.

Blue Sky's work so far has shown how, in our time, the principles of Arts and Crafts Modernism can be brought to houses on the West Coast and enriched. There is an obvious echo of Charles and Henry Greene, particularly in the most recent work. But Blue Sky would never stoop to make mock hardwood beams round softwood structures as the Greenes did (nor to using concealed steels like Frank Lloyd Wright and, yes, it has to be admitted, even the architectural grandfather of the whole Arts and Crafts Movement, Philip Webb). What you see and feel in a Blue Sky building is real.

Helliwell and Smith are inheritors and interpreters of the Organic tradition of Modernism. But they are free of its often claustrophobic tendencies. Scharoun's domestic plans, for instance, scarcely allow users much freedom: either you are sitting there, looking at that view, or you have to go to the dining table or to bed. Conversely, Blue Sky has avoided the mainstream Modernist reaction to organic specificity: bland, undifferentiated space. Blue Sky's volumes certainly flow into each other, but they form an interconnected tissue of internal and external places, simultaneously specific and capable of many individual interpretations.

The buildings are kindly, and tender to humankind and nature, which are both enriched by their existence. We look forward to a new phase in the life of the practice, in which urban buildings will be added to the country houses. The extension will be difficult. But I have no doubt that it will succeed. And teach us much about how the noble and generous sensibilities of Hornby Island and the accumulated experience of Blue Sky can be extended to a wider world.

PETER DAVEY
Peter Davey is the Editor of *The Architectural Review*, London and author of *The Arts and Crafts Movement*

CONTENTS

INTRODUCTION

by Trevor Boddy

After the pure joy of touring the houses collected in this book, nestled as they are into landscapes of startling beauty and variety, there soon came the more difficult task of finding a vocabulary to write of them. Strewn through my first notes on the houses, and the design connections between them, these three descriptors came up time and again: 'picturesque,' 'tectonic' and 'romantic.' I feel these three qualities are very useful in understanding the local and international accomplishments of Bo Helliwell and Kim Smith's fairly new firm, and that singly and together they constitute an attitude towards nature. Moreover, this trio also describe the increasingly distinctive quality of the best of Canadian architecture in general, and show that Helliwell + Smith are part of a broader movement. At the risk of pedantry, some indications of what I mean by these three words, and how they might apply to the houses in this book:

PICTURESQUE—While architects have always composed their buildings visually, by the 18th into the early 19th centuries, especially in Britain and its colonial empire, architects had come further to compose buildings pictorially, incorporating features specifically to create picture-like effects. Aesthetic theories of the 'Sublime and the Terrible' also brought architecture into a new relationship with the raw power of nature. These are at the essence of the house designs of Helliwell + Smith, which are always designed to work with minimally-modified natural sites, are conceived with views to and from them as one of their principal design generators, and favour a repertoire of detail that demonstrates a belief in architecture as a middle term between culture and nature.

TECTONIC—This refers to the builderly, constructed quality of houses, the issues that arise out of the physical making of buildings, and a conception of design which renders these important goals in their own right, not just instrumental means to an end. Above these conceptions, associated with Anglo-American theorist and critic Kenneth Frampton, there is another fortunate association of the work: plate tectonics

and the creation and change of landforms. What sets the houses of Helliwell + Smith from those in most architectural publications today is the degree to which their plans, elevations and especially sections are conceived in continuation or pointed counterpoint to surrounding landforms—what I later call a dialogue of building with landscape—each inconceivable without the other after construction is complete. Both Kim Smith and Bo Helliwell have backgrounds as builders, and even though they no longer build their own designs, they have an unsually intimate and productive relationship with construction crews and contractors, who often carry through from project to project. They tend to treat what their typical architectural colleagues usually regard as mere contractual obligations into much richer atelier-like collaborations with builders, and consequently receive unusually strong cooperation and praise from the teams they lead. This all results in the high level of constructional care and consistency evident throughout their finished houses.

ROMANTIC—As a culture, Canada developed under the influence of literary and painterly romanticism in the 19th century. An icy kind of passion links the paintings of our Group of Seven, the music and writings of Glenn Gould, the films of Atom Agoyan and Robert Lepage, the poetry and novels of Margaret Atwood and Michael Ondaatje, the songwriting of Leonard Cohen and Joni Mitchell. The houses of Helliwell + Smith share some of these qualities, nearly always carrying a surprising emotional wallop only passingly evoked by the plans and photographs collected here. Peter Davey's Preface has captured the utopian romanticism of Hornby Island, the crucible of hopes for new ways of living that shapes their design today long after Helliwell + Smith have moved to Vancouver, and applies to houses no matter where they are now constructed. This romanticism comes with a price, however, being embarrassingly revealing and uniquely committed in an era when modish cynicism and provisional vetements have become the surest means to an architectural reputation.

A key late work of the First Vancouver School, Erickson-Massey's 1964 Smith House II in West Vancouver

With the picturesque, the tectonic and the romantic as the locus of interpretation of their work, some background on the context of local architectural history and culture, the landscapes where they work, and biographies for both of the architects is needed for richer appreciation of their accomplishments and vulnerabilities. For a century and more, British Columbia has been the location of some of the most sublimely innovative houses and housing in all of North America. The British Arts and Crafts Movement took hold here as nowhere else on the continent, a legacy of both our still-colonial outlook in the province at the turn of the century, and the immediacy of craft in wood amidst forests as powerful as any on earth. With the turn to Modernism in the 1940s and 1950s, architects here continued the best of the arts and crafts philosophy but celebrated structure and space over surface and finish, transforming walls into windows and breaking down the barriers between indoor and outdoor, a needed rush of light in a mild, grey, remote place only starting to realize its potential.

This Modernist 'First Vancouver School' of B.C. Binning, Arthur Erickson, Ron Thom and Fred Hollinsworth has been superceded by the current 'Second Vancouver School,' informally consisting of architects like Peter Cardew, Roger Hughes and John and Patricia Patkau, architects who—like Helliwell and Smith, make a dialogue with nature and with landform a fundamental component of their internationally-acclaimed designs. Indeed, the trio of the picturesque, the tectonic and the romantic might just as surely be applied to most works by both First and Second Vancouver Schools. Looming over all of these are the memory and continuing presence of the monumental carvings, masks, totem poles and especially cedar planked houses of the native Indians of British Columbia, whose material culture is 'the equal of anything produced in Renaissance Italy or Imperial China' according to anthropologist Claude Levi-Straus, who studied it after writing 'Tristes Tropiques.'

With an extremely mountainous terrain, buildable land has always been expensive here, absurdly so in booming Vancouver, both the densest city on the continent (only a few Manhattan neighbourhoods have higher dwelling densities than Vancouver's downtown peninsula) but also its youngest, the city having been effectively invented as a land promotion scheme by the Canadian Pacific Railway in 1883. In Vancouver, the best architects still do houses and housing. This is much different than the situation elsewhere in Canada and the United States, where domestic design has been relegated to a modestly para-professional mode, punctuated occasionally and noisily when architects of public and commercial buildings deign to design a trophy house for a designer-collecting client.

Amongst the best of our best architects who continue to create houses are partners-in-design and in-life Kim Smith and Bo Helliwell. In a hectic decade since founding their practice and joint household, they have produced a corpus of homes that have garnered architectural and building industry awards from around Canada, along the way producing several exhibitions of their work, and have lectured in Europe and the Americas. They maintain studio-office-homes in West Vancouver, Hornby Island and Whistler, and their life is a non-stop hejira of design work and enjoyment of nature in these three stunningly different locales. They enjoy the constant commuting by car and ferry amongst this lushly archipeligoed triad, and dialogues with the architects while passing through some of the most sublime maritime and alpine landscapes in the world with them has produced some of the most insightful and honest observations about the work collected here.

Hornby Island's Helliwell Park, named for a distant relative of Bo

The Helliwell + Smith houses from the last decade collected here have been carefully chosen by us from several dozen more in order to chart the evolution of their design ideas, and to demonstrate, for instance, how the contingencies of the instant ski resort of Whistler produce fundamentally different houses than those for the well-worn southern Gulf Islands, even while they share a building repertoire of similar shapes, details and embellishments. At the end of the portfolio of these houses—which contain descriptive and critical texts from the architects and me—there are appendices which include unbuilt house projects and a number of inspirational houses codesigned by Helliwell in his previous firm, Blue Sky Design. Because Bo Helliwell and Kim Smith came together in mid-career, it is important to describe each of their training and design experiences before the commencement of their partnership, along the way introducing the remarkable places where they choose to build.

Bo Helliwell Biography

Born in 1944 to a department store manager and nurse, Bo Helliwell spent most of his youth in what is now known as Thunder Bay, Ontario. Visually and functionally the link between the Canadian prairies and the St. Lawrence Seaway, the town is dominated by an astonishing row of cast concrete grain elevators, the type that Le Corbusier praised as 'the first fruits of the new era' of Modernism in *'Towards a New Architecture.'* While these were a favoured destination for young Helliwell's winter skating adventures, these architectural delights could not compete with the lessons from nature taught by spending summers at a family lakeside cottage 'where we used to chase bears on our bikes'. His first direct contact with architecture came with the discovery of an old set of blueprints, which intrigued him for their graphic quality and sense of a world in miniature. Before he was 10 Bo Helliwell was announcing that he would one day be an architect, despite never having met one.

That would happen with a family move to Winnipeg when he was 15, where a number of neighbours were architects in this much larger city, including the highly respected Dean of the University of Manitoba's School of Architecture, John Russell. Beginning in the 1930s, Russell had built Manitoba into Canada's most advanced and rigourous citadel of Modernism, with Sydney's Harry Seidler and Toronto's John C. Parkin amongst his early protégés. Russell's son, Barry, was soon amongst Helliwell's best friends, and he spent much time in their house, surrounded by a superb art and architecture library and original works of art: 'they were so much more cultured than anyone I had met before' Helliwell says.

Duly inspired, he was admitted to the University of Manitoba's School of Architecture, spending his summers working in the slide library instead of better-paying construction jobs because of the opportunity for further enrichment that a knowledge of art history offered him. With first year studio having Bauhaus-derived graphic exercises in formal composition, his second year building design came under the influence of Gustavo Da Roza, who gained much respect from students for the Modernist houses he was then building in a neighbourhood appropriately named Tuxedo Park. Only now realizing how much there was to learn in architecture, Helliwell got as far as lining up to register for third year, but abandoned it, convinced he needed to get some practical experience.

Helliwell was soon working for Etienne Gaboury, where he remained for the academic year, then continued in summers after. While also a Modernist, Gaboury had a wider palette of forms and symbols operating in his architecture than the formalist Da Roza, most evident in his own riverside house and the spiral-formed Eglise du Précieux Sang in a francophone Winnipeg suburb. The late 1960s and early 1970s were a time of considerable ferment in Canadian architecture, especially on the prairies, where the example of EXPO 67 and a heady dose of nationalism for the Centennial of Canadian 'confederation' (independence from Britian) which it celebrated combined to up the cultural importance for architecture, and gave architects considerable latitude for formy innovation. Upon a curving brick base wrapping the ground floor, Précieux Sang is a striking helix form of glu-lam beams rising above the altar, its curving exterior surfaces covered with cedar shakes. Echoes of this 1969 building are seen in Blue Sky's 1982 Saks' house in Hornby. Renewed and emboldened by the experience with Gaboury, Helliwell continued his studies at Manitoba to emerge by graduation as one of the top designers in his class.

'Eglise du Précieux Sang' by architect Etienne Gaboury 1967

In the summer of 1968 Helliwell headed for San Francisco and Haight-Ashbury, like much of his generation. A 'summer of love' it was not to be, as while stopping in Vancouver to visit an aunt he quickly landed a job with Canada's most famous and influential architectural firm, Erickson and Massey. Their competition-winning Simon Fraser University design had been completed and published to global acclaim, and the magnificent Smith House of 1964 demonstrated a renewal of the Vancouver romantic Modernist house tradition with the infusion of tectonic ideas from monumental post-and-beam construction ideas of the Haida, Kwakiutl and other northwest native groups. Helliwell worked closely with Geoff Massey on custom houses, and his earliest Blue Sky designs, such as the Graham House, featured in an appendix at the end of this book, clearly show the legacy of Erickson-Massey's domestic work on the creations of Blue Sky Design.

During his 1968-72 period at Erickson-Massey, Helliwell completed his first designs for the new ski resort town of Whistler, notably the Moore Lyndon Turner Whittaker Sea Ranch-influenced Rothstein House (by then Helliwell had finally made it to California and a tour of this hugely influential and eminently picturesque-tectonic-romantic rural development), with its angular roofs, 'saddle-bag' cantilevered rooms, and board-covered elevations. His first constructed design, the Rothstein house was so highly regarded within the Erickson-Massey office that they put it forward as one of their submissions to Canada's highest architectural award. While the house did not win, Helliwell had gained experience working directly with clients and designing and supervising the construction of a house, the first phase in his apprenticeship now completed.

Rothstein House 1970, Whistler designed by Bo Helliwell at Erickson Massey

Kim Smith Biography

While 10 years younger, Kim Smith has brought rich architectural experience of her own and a whole new range of formal and intellectual concerns to their shared work in the partnership. Smith and Helliwell share a rare life and design partnership where differing backgrounds and views—even senses of space—invigorate their work; without question, they design better together than either did in their previous careers. While they have different senses of space, detail and colour, Helliwell + Smith are linked at the more important level of design philosophy and architectural ethos, which I have described as a commitment to the picturesque, the tectonic and the romantic. Smith's strength and independence is best understood by an account of her extended training and early architectural experience.

Kim Smith was born in Kingston, Ontario in 1953, the middle of three children. With an artistic mother and a civil engineer-turned-land-developer father, she grew up much inspired by the possibilities of creative making. A true child of suburbia, she grew up in an unusual Modernist house designed by an interior designer; unusual in this four-square, brickish Ontario town for having an A-frame living room and exposed woodwork and beams in Douglas fir. Queen's University is widely regarded as Canada's finest small university, and Smith received a B.A. double major in English and Film Studies there in 1976. She first came to western Canada for some final coursework at UBC, and continued her early interests in sailing, skiing and hiking with renewed vigour in the west. Exposure to building came as she helped shoot film footage of the construction of a solar house on Vancouver Island for the National Film Board.

She returned to Ontario temporarily to rent a farm near Napanee with a friend, planning while there to build a 40-foot catamaran and sail it back to British Columbia by way of the Caribbean, a lifelong dream ever since she learned to sail on Lake Ontario. 'We were being earth people' says Smith wryly 'wood stoves, fingerless gloves, lots of cold and damp in an Ontario winter.' Earth people with a Utopian mission, however, as construction soon began on a 60 by 40 foot boat shed, the first building she designed and built. Limited budget also meant lots of improvisation of construction detail for the catamaran as well. After nearly two years of construction, the voyage was as improvised as the construction. 'We couldn't afford ocean charts, so we had to use advanced dead reckoning—backed up with standard road maps—to sail across New York State along the Erie Canal then down the Eastern Seaboard.' The catamaran and the relationship that produced it 'Both got shipwrecked as we entered the Caribbean, so I came back to British Columbia to tree plant and reconsider my life.'

She soon applied for admission to the School of Architecture at Vancouver's University of British Columbia, the catamaran and construction shed the focus of her design/drawing portfolio. She was admitted to the school in fall of 1980, and soon bought a house with friends. Through her first two years of study she renovated a house for communal living then radically renovated a 10 by 16 foot coach-house for herself behind it. I first met Kim while a sessional lecturer at UBC during this period, and came to appreciate her drive, thoughfulness and skill, all apparent when I toured her coach-house with a student group, as the building had range of detail, a warmth of texture and colour, and an ease of occupation which spoke of a much more sophisticated designer than a second year student.

Except for some of us occasional lecturers, the UBC architecture school of the early 1980s had very strong links to the Universities of Oregon and Berkeley, and to the nurturing of unconventional lifestyles and alternative politics associated with Eugene, Oregon and Berkeley's Telegraph Avenue. Christopher Alexander's *'A Pattern Language'* was virtually the design manual for first year design studio, but the school had surprisingly little to do with Canada's finest collection of architects in practice downtown, and design-oriented professors like Arthur Erickson and Bruno Freschi were pushed out after getting major commissions, never to return.

Smith opted to spend her summers tree planting rather than work for firms, in part because she had so few female role models at UBC and in the world of architecture generally: 'We had no female studio faculty, and few in the magazines or offices.' Her final thesis was as full of conviction, passion and design imagination as any I have seen in a decade of full-time studio teaching. Conceived just at the cusp of non-gay awareness of the AIDS crisis, her thesis was a rigorously programmatic, artfully planned, straightforwardly presented sex club, with rooms, features and zones for every and all preferences. 'Building on my film background I wanted something that involved play and fantasy, and it was a time of questioning sex and gender roles.' While there was something of a 'punk aesthetic' to the plan and an *'épater les bourgeois'* chutzpah of the very idea of a sex club, it was compelling for its conviction and thoroughness, and Smith soon graduated into an uncertain market for young architects. The jagged geometries of the sex club, with low walls to zone adjacent uses appears in the Gadsby house and many other subsequent designs with Helliwell, so even its forms live on, if not the tenor of the times that produced it.

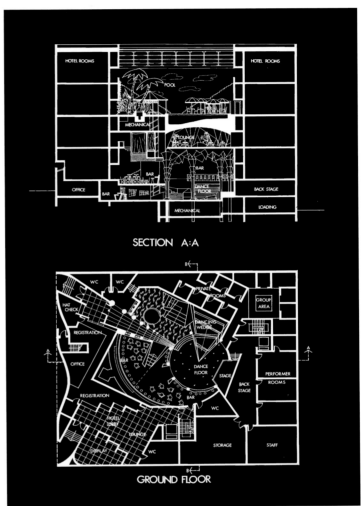

'Love Hotel' thesis by Kim Smith 1984

By 1984 Vancouver was at the nadir of one of its cyclic recessions, still being a city and province hugely dependent on natural resource commodity price swings. Smith was soon doing pavilion interiors for the upcoming EXPO 86, this frustrating experience convincing her that she would like to complete her education and work for herself, instead. In summer of 1985 she attended a summer studio at the Pratt Institute in New York City, but elected to change to the Architectural Association School in London's Bedford Square that fall, all the while working for highly regarded Anglo-Canadian London architect Trevor Horne, mainly on domestic projects.

'Jungle Room', The Licks Restaurant 1987 by Kim Smith and Niki Kozakavitch

Having the credentials she needed from UBC and the supplementary education she desired from the AA, Smith left after one year in London, eager to return to Canada's west coast. She soon bought a house on Hornby which she renovated while working independently in Vancouver, along the way collaborating with Nicki Kozakavitch to design a remarkable jungle 'theme' restaurant in West Vancouver, a since-renovated room announcing the themes of all of her subsequent work: bold colour, a playful spatial sense, a seductiveness of surface and texture. Soon working for AA-trained designer Tony Robbins, she was spending more and more time on Hornby, a romance now developing after years of friendship with Bo. Soon they were living and working together, and later, married. Starting with the Stewart and Gadsby houses, they also married their approaches to design, evident in the portfolio of projects which follows.

Conclusion

It is tempting to view the work of Helliwell + Smith as a direct extension of the 'wood-butcher's aesthetic' of Hornby Island and other counter-cultural refuges across the western mountains and deserts of North America, and their equivalents in Australia, Southeast Asia and Europe. For the later work, these connections are more apparent than real. Of the projects arrayed in the next section of this book, none were built by them, even though they remain committed to a tectonic conception of architecture and maintain a romantic belief in a community of builders.

Similarly, 'green' or 'organic' architecture seems to offer some parallels to their work. But this is confounded by Helliwell + Smith treating nature as more a visual system than one where energy concerns dominate, resulting in the ultimately picturesque nature of their designs (pictorially conceived out of a concern for views to and from) rather than a truly organic approach, with its direct mimesis of nature and sublimation of forms into a nested geometric order. The only exception to this might be the work of eccentric Los Angeles' domestic architect John Lautner, who Helliwell and Smith met late in his life, and whose work they toured thoroughly.

By means of contrast, a comparison with Vancouver colleagues and friends John and Patricia Patkau is useful, architects who also build houses on spectacular west coast sites, using a similar combination of intellectuality, formal invention, and deference to local building and site conditions. Their Patkau's Barnes house in Nanaimo, Pyrch house in Victoria, and their own West Vancouver residence are all spectacular, but tend to be in suburban areas rather than Blue Sky's more remote Gulf Islands and the resort town of Whistler. The Patkau's work is more restrictively Modern in inspiration, while Helliwell + Smith is softer in the most positive sense, permitting a wider range of design sources and allusions.

Australian domestic design of the 1980s and 1990s—especially that of Glenn Murcutt—is a more useful comparison. Murcutt's work also is much more complex and cerebral upon examination and inhabitation than it appears when passively consumed as images. Brit Andresen/Peter O'Gorman, Lindsay Clare and Murcutt have the same edgy relationship to interpretations of their work as solely regionalist as do Helliwell + Smith. For both Australians and Canadians, a commitment to working with indigenous materials, and respecting local regimes of light and landscape does not mean filtering out formal ideas and foreign precedent, but rather the more demanding task of reiterating these in the means at hand, of making the general specific. It also seems to me my trio of the picturesque, the tectonic and the romantic are as present in the best Australian domestic design as Canadian, and for many of the same historic and intellectual reasons, but this exploration is for another book.

These types of comparisons can only be provisional, and Helliwell + Smith must finally be evaluated on their own terms, but informed also by the views of their clients—those necessary participants in the intimate act which is the design of a custom house. What struck me most in talking with many of their clients in preparing this essay was the continuing delight they take in discovering new features—a special play of light, a new use for a nook, a link to land or nature not previously understood—up to a decade after first occupying their houses. These houses often have a subtly didactic quality, teaching quiet but profound lessons about our visual relationship to the natural world, a Socratic dialogue between the shape of rooms and walls and the landscape beyond. Were mere geometric formalism or shifting contemporary detail to solely inform their work,

Helliwell + Smith might be better known in the magazine-publishable or 'here's a look for our art museum' sense, but they are strong in their commitment to instead work with the hopes and imaginings of clients, voiced or not, in dialogue with a natural world whose visual wisdom is profound. For a private house, no greater intellectual or architectural ambition is possible.

"Trevor Boddy
Hornby Island and Vancouver, fall 1998"

Trevor Boddy is a Vancouver architectural historian, critic and consultant. With a Master's degree in architecture from the University of Calgary, he has taught at the universities of Oregon, Manitoba, Toronto and British Columbia, published criticism in most of the world's leading design magazines, and lectured globally on contemporary Canadian architecture. His critical monograph *The Architecture of Douglas Cardinal* was named 'Alberta Book of the Year' and short-listed for an International Union of Architects prize for criticism. He is also the author of *Modern Architecture in Alberta* and contributed the chapter 'Underground and Overhead: Building the Analogous City' in *Variations on a Theme Park: the New American City and the End of Public Space* named one of the most important books of 1992 by the Voice Literary Supplement of New York.

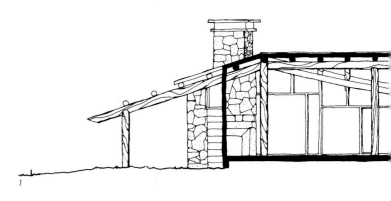

1

GREENWOOD HOUSE

Design 1993/Completion 1996
3,000-sq.ft. house
Galiano Island, B.C.

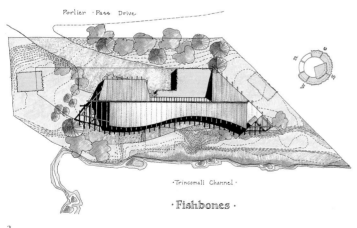

2

3

The name for this house evolved into 'Fishbones', not a metaphor we began with but one which evolved with solving the contingencies of a narrow site wedged between road and rocky shore. The shoreline on the north end of Galiano Island is smooth molded sandstone, here mounted by irregular large rocks, with powerfully rugged century-old Garry Oaks rising up out of nooks and crannies. The sensuality of the sandstone beach generated the curving and sensuous lines of this house both in plan and section.

The potential buildable site is a small shelf tightly constrained by setback requirements from both high tide line, and the main island road which passes by above. Given this, it was natural that the house be conceived of as an outgrowth of the land and water.

Working mainly in model, we devised a 'backbone' ridge beam of 14' diameter cedar logs parallel to the shore, interlaced with 9' diameter log rafters set at various angles to form the view—exploiting plan-linked undulations of the roof. This rafter structure extends beyond the roof at both ends revealing the skeleton and bringing the house back to the ground. A continuous skylight runs along the spine in order that the bright sunlight reflected off the ocean side is balanced by a more coolly diffused forest light at the centre of the main rooms. The post and beam structure combined with the undulations of spaces in plan and section created the illusion of the skeletal remains of a salmon and the name 'Fishbones' was born.

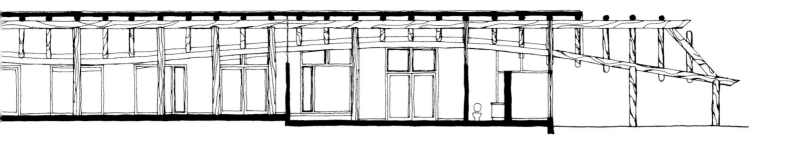

4

We see this house as a further evolution in our work, it combines a strong rational structural rhythm defined by log posts and rafters with a less geometric and more organic based form in plan and section reminiscent of the work of John Lautner. The building of the house was a successful example in our philosophic approach to building, a creative partnership between ourselves, the owner Barry Greenwood and the builder Alan Fletcher.

Barry and Sofia Greenwood were living in Jakarta during the design and construction of the house and brought to it a magnificent range of carved tropical wood antiques from Java and Bali, along with a desire for Japanese

tatami and *shoji* screens in their bedroom. With cherry planking and slate covered radiant heated slab flooring and a wide range of custom details in wood, the house had to be able to provide a suitable location for their collection without distracting from the powerful visuals of prime nature all around.

Continued...

1 *Longitudinal section*
2 *Site plan*
3 *Study model 'Fishbones'*
4 *West elevation*

Boddy

There is a highly differentiated plan order in the Fishbones House, with squared off forms containing garage and children's bedrooms on the developed roadside, and a sinuous curve on the water side of the main inhabited spaces. While these choices could compete and even conflict, the strong visual link of the roof structure provides a seductive continuity to the interior sequence of rooms, each differing angle of the rafters drawing visitors from entrance, through gallery-kitchen to the living-room,

terminated by a massive fireplace. Less obvious, but just as significant a design decision here are the siteworks. Despite their naturalistic detailing, the stone plinth upon which the house sits is all designed and constructed, with the deck forming the most important 'room' of the house. The strength, weight and modesty of these decisions provides the perfect foil to the airy organicism of the Fishbones metaphor, rendering more impressive the roof structure's flight of uninhibited fancy.

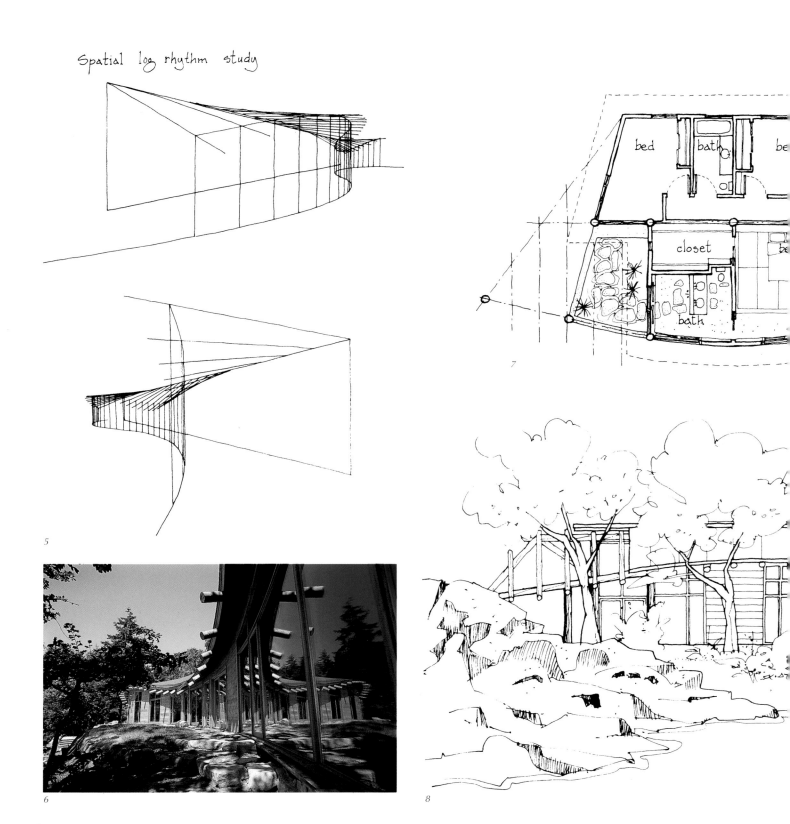

Spatial log rhythm study

5

bed bath be

closet be

bath

7

6

8

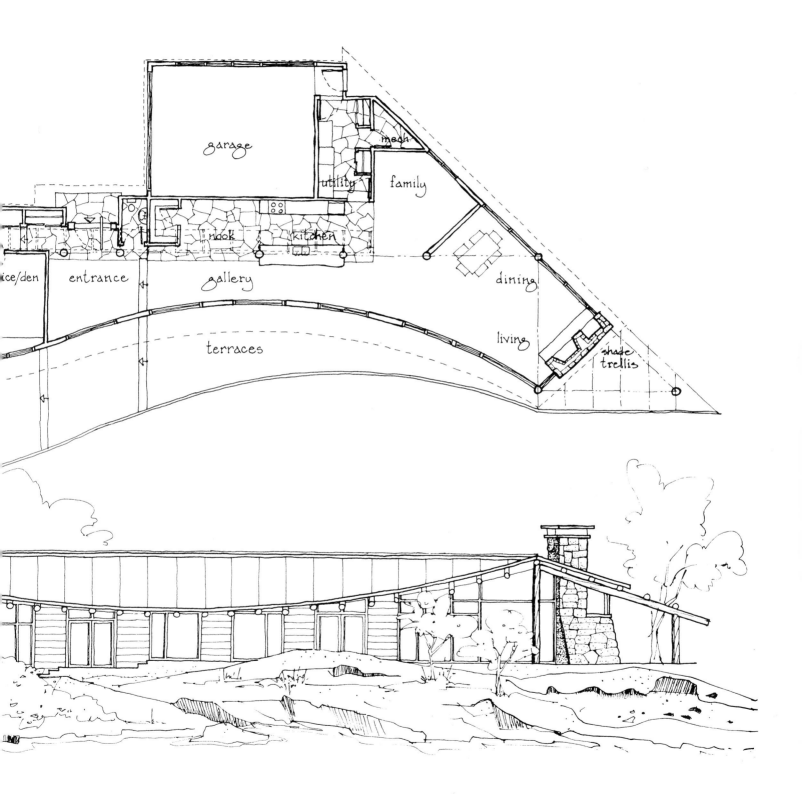

garage

mech

utility

family

nook

kitchen

ice/den

entrance

gallery

dining

terraces

living

shade trellis

9

9   Roadside view
10   Northwest terrace
11   Oceanside view
12   Post and beam connection detail

10

11

12

13

14

15

13   *Sandstone bluffs—form generator*
14   *Post and beam—light detail*
15   *Site visit, Kim Smith, Bo Helliwell*
Opposite:
    Interior gallery

18

19

20

Previous pages:
   Living room
18 Sandstone fireplace
19 Entry gallery
20 Kitchen and nook
21 Dining room
22 Bedroom
23 Interior gallery looking north

21

22

23

HARVEY HOUSE

Design 1995/Completion 1996
2,200-sq.ft. house
Denman Island, B.C.

1

Denman Island is flatter, tamer and more agricultural than adjacent Hornby Island. Jim and Barbara Harvey bought this site, a fairly flat section of seashore overlooking Baynes Sound on the west side of the island, to develop both a retirement home for themselves and a family centre. Barbara brought to the project a European Modernist eye from her Berlin background, while Jim brought his strong environmentalist sensitivity. They were both concerned that the house be economical while fulfilling their needs and aesthetics. This and their desire to have the house work as a backdrop to their many antique furniture pieces, contributed to the simplicity found in this house.

When we first surveyed the site we noticed a trail that has long been worn for access by Denman Islanders to the sand and gravel beach below. We decided to respect this pathway by bridging the house over it. The plan is long and linear with all major rooms stretched parallel to the ocean to maximize views and light. The metaphor of bridge is used in two ways in the house; one, with the house literally bridging over the existing pathway and two, with a trestle structure that forms and supports the long curving roof form that arches across the house. Although we have used this post, beam and raftered structure to create curving roofs in previous houses, this is the purest and simplest expression of that structural idea to date. Filtered light from the forest penetrates clerestory windows above the eastern wall to balance the western light reflecting off the sea. Most of the structure for the house is milled from trees removed to build the house and much of the existing forest is still intact with several trees coming through the new decks and terraces.

2

3

Boddy

This house is a recent breakthrough for the career of Helliwell + Smith, recognized in its receipt of an Award of Honour in the 1998 Canadian Wood Council design awards, and a 1998 Lieutenant Governor's Award in British Columbia. The house is remarkable for the clarity of the concept, plan, section and structure, all organized around a bridge metaphor that does not compromise inhabitation, but provides a framework for its disposition. While many of their previous houses have highly variegated plans, with each particularization in plan, a wall seemingly as important as the other (sometimes thereby canceling out their impact and import), there is a clear hierarchy of plan here, with the concave front, for instance, clearly subservient to the larger symmetrical plan form and sailing roof form. Helliwell + Smith have seldom designed a roof structure as powerful as this, but more importantly, never so well integrated it into the plan and spatial character of a residence—a mature design, and one which may prefigure a more placidly classical plan conception in future work.

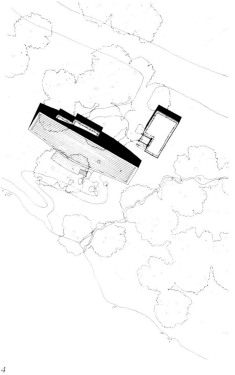

4

1   Beach front—Baynes Sound
2   Beachside elevation
3   Construction shot
4   Site plan

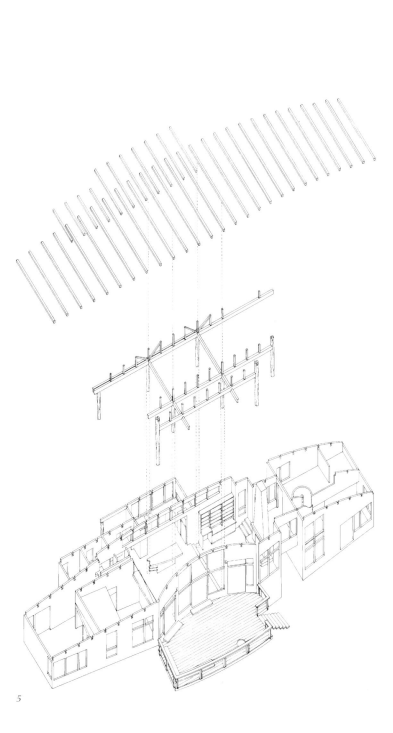

5

6

7

5 Exploded axonometric
6 Roadside elevation from northeast
7 West elevation and terrace
8 Garden elevation and bridge detail

8

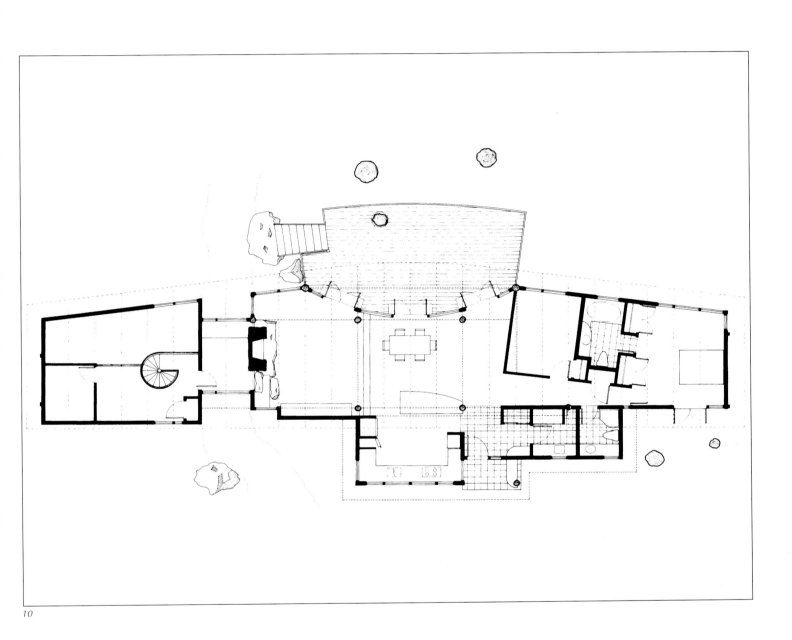

10

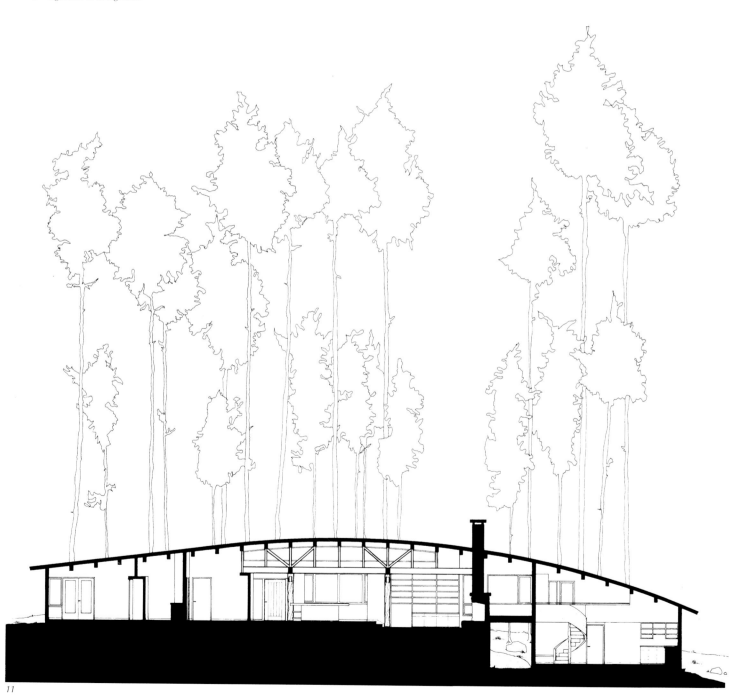

11

12

13

14

15

MIKES BARON HOUSE

Design 1995/Construction 1996
3,000-sq.ft. house
Whistler, B.C.

The site for this house is in the mountain area of Whistler, with varied topography including a beautiful platform of sculpted granite, great views and light to the east and crown land forest to the west. The owners of the house are both naturalists with strong environmental aesthetics. It was important to them that the house both have and appear to have minimal impact on the site. We approached the design both with this sensibility in mind and a play with metaphors drawn from their lives. For him—a river rafting guide—we used a river (the curving plan form through granite outcrop) and for her—a naturalist and bird expert—we used a bird house (their bedroom bay perched on a massive single log post).

A section was developed to straddle the existing granite outcrop, dropping below it at the back of the site towards the forest. The plan of the main social spaces embraces the granite outcrop and simple shed roofs over the social spaces and sleeping wing rise in opposing slopes. The structure for the great room is a simple post and beam based on a radial geometry from a centre point on the granite outcrop. The wood post and beam structure is extremely heavy supporting a combined snow load and a grass roof of 400 lb./sq.ft. expressed as such. A single large natural tree trunk in the main space acts like the post in a *tokinoma*, expressing the wild and natural in a cultivated setting. The main roof is covered in grass, creating the only cultivated landscape as well as a gesture of healing the site.

Boddy

This house has an intimacy and warmth in large part because its permanent resident clients— a wilderness tour operator and a naturalist/ writer—wanted to avoid the self-conscious and sybaritic 'trophy houses' that many occasional Whistler visitors demand. This said, there is a powerful sweep and grandeur to this house, especially its arrival and entrance sequence, a sublime *esquisse* in architectural choreography.

Continued...

1

1 Axonometric
2 East elevation
3 South elevation
4 Second floor plan
5 First floor plan
6 East elevation in snow
7 Construction shot

2

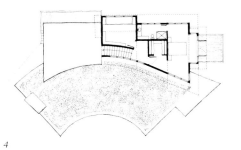

4

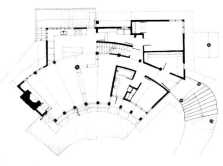

5

3

6

7

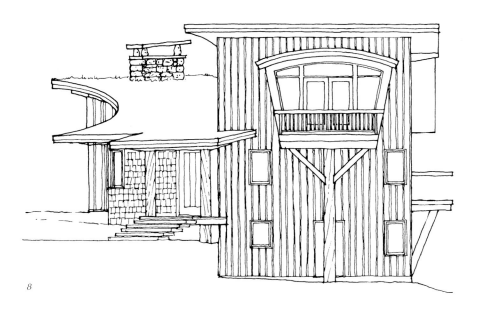

8

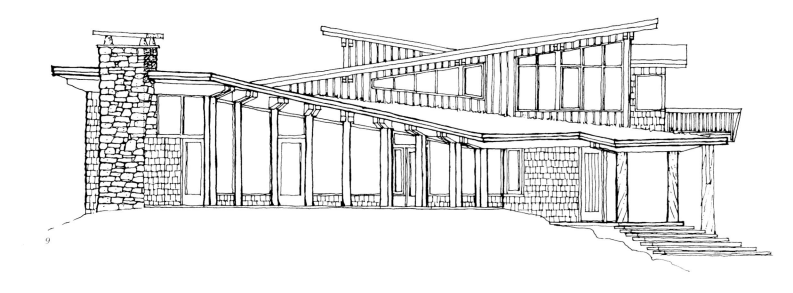

9

From the driveway one passes round a massive rock out-cropping, the curving elevation rotating around in a perfect *pas-de-deux* on the other side, particularly impressive with night-time up-lighting which emphasizes the massive but elegant post-and-beam order. Once inside, a more feminine presence intervenes, with an enticing waltz up a curving corridor that rises in sections, its path marked by custom alabaster light fixtures perched on radially-set columns, enticing oblique views to the high kitchen windows beckoning above. After the enclosure and separation of the corridor, the main living/dining/kitchen space erupts into fully spatial dance with the double beams rotating in plan and advancing in section above, the windows in *contre-poise*, the chrome yellow wall colours watching and calling back, the fireplace laughing heartily, and finally the original rock outcropping now viewed anew as the glowering presence from an earlier act. Yet for all this spatial action, attention is inevitably set on the frozen dynamism of a sinuous log-column, bark removed to reveal intriguing curving maze patterns created by a previous *corps-de-beetles*, a kind of dance within the dancer.

10

8　North elevation
9　East elevation
10　'Bird House'

11　East elevation in snow
12　Curve of roof in snow
Opposite:
　　Living room to dining room

11

12

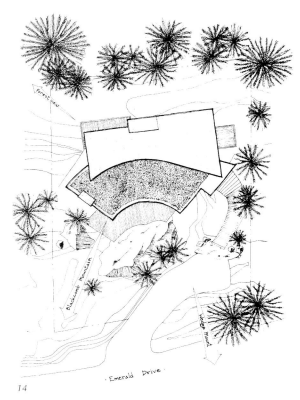

14

14   Site plan
15   View to kitchen and dining room
     from living room
16   View to kitchen
17   View from hall
18   View to living room

15

16

17

18

19

20

19 Bedroom bay
20 Dining room to living room
21 Library window bay
22 Fireplace detail with Narwhale tusk and bones

21

22

COLLINS' HOUSE

Design 1995/Construction 1996
3,500-sq.ft. house
Whistler, B.C.

1

Stretching along the top of a ridge with magnificent mountain views to the east and west, this site is in the middle of a subdivision of holiday homes in the ski resort of Whistler. Glen and Julie Collins wanted a vacation home that would endure as a family gathering place for all seasons.

Our strategy with the site was to stretch the house lengthwise on the property so that we could capitalize on mountain views at both ends, and because of the long thin plan, we were able to save a small grove of pine trees on the south side. We used two different approaches for fenestration, one at the ends of the house was windows as frames for the breathtaking views, while another with windows with long vertical louvres on the sides of the house to allow light and ventilation as well as screening from the neighbours.

In this house we used low sloped curving roof forms, recalling the metaphor of snow drifts. The low sloped roof form covered in copper sheds snow while allowing upper floors views beyond it. The house has an expressed base clad in river rock granite, with a heavy textured cedar board siding above. A mix of rustic and refined materials blend to define the wild and cultivated nature of a ski resort.

Boddy

One of the larger houses collected in this volume, the Collins' house has a scale and volume unusual in the range of Helliwell + Smith's domestic work. Much of this is due to the pressure on house sizes that comes from a limited number of building sites in one of the most exclusive and fast-growing winter resorts in the world. There is a widespread desire to maximize an architectural investment that can only appreciate dramatically, and this house is a weekend house built to the maximum permitted by Whistler's planning regulations, 3,500 square feet, its apparent size amplified further by very generous floor-to-floor heights.

The best features of the house are at its perimeters, where the front and back elevations exploit Wagnerian alpine views, and clever detailing of the stair and dining room fenestration integrate light without losing privacy to flanking houses on either side. A column-free and huge-windowed master bedroom is achieved with quirky trusses of vertically-hung king post compression members and steel cable tension members sheathed in an ornamental copper tube. The shallow curved vault of the ceiling is thus permitted to run unencumbered to windows as big as the mountains they overlook. Aalto-esque over-scaled vertical fin-mullions at stair landings and dining room windows not only gather bounced light without compromising privacy, but also provide needed scale and dimensionality to the otherwise indeterminate spaces at the centre of the plan on main living levels.

2

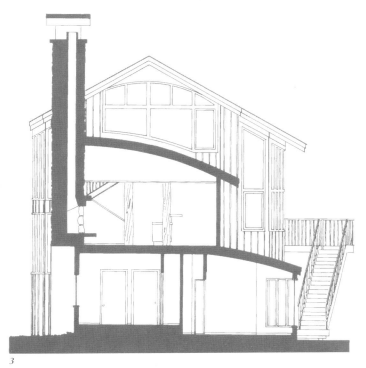

3

1   Street elevation in snow
2   East elevation
3   Section
4   Street elevation in summer

4

5

5   Main stair and kitchen
6   South elevation
7   Upstairs bridge

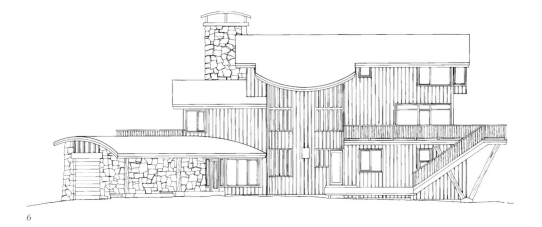

6

7

8

8   Light detail above dining room
9   Site plan
10   Dining room

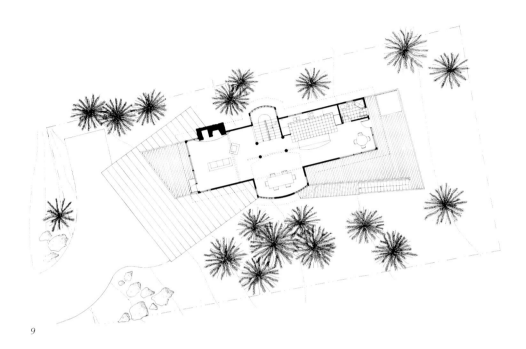

9

10

11

11   View from living room
12   Bedroom bay and truss
13   View from bedroom

12

13

ROCHE HOUSE

Design 1992/Construction 1993
2,400-sq.ft. house
Whistler, B.C.

1

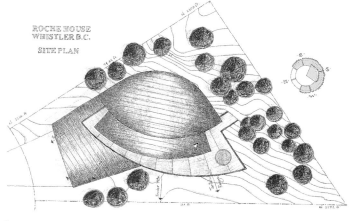

2

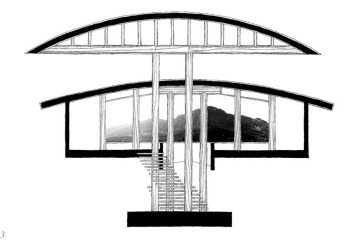

3

As with many sites in the mountainous area of Whistler, this site was extremely steep with a restricted building footprint. The house form was generated by sectional concerns; how to get light into the areas buried into the hillside and how to integrate the house vertically, socially, visually, spatially and audially. We used a grand stair framed by a two- and three-story fir post and beam structure to connect the three levels, through movement, space and light. Clerestory windows in the third story main bedroom throw light through the second floor living area down to the main entry on the first floor.

The first floor is expressed as a solid base with punched windows into bedrooms. The second and third floors have curved sloping roofs that shed snow with a relatively low slope that allows light into the spaces above.

Covered in snow they appear as soft sculpted snowdrifts in the landscape. This house is also the first time we used structural log posts in a window wall as seen in the front wall of the living and dining rooms. We also extended our vocabulary of post and beam structure with varied lengths of uprights supported on beams that support roof joists and create the curved roofs.

The house was built as a recreation family home in the ski resort of Whistler.

Boddy

The Roche house is one of the most compact and delightful combinations of constructional rigour and spatial glamour produced to date by Helliwell + Smith. Much of this was achieved through a turn to enriching sections

1   Post and beam detail at entrance
2   Site plan
3   Structural parti
4   Street elevation
5   Stair from entry
6   Street entrance

5

4

6

from the hyper-responsive plans of the Gulf Island houses, most of them variations on single levels. Richer qualities of light and overlook are achieved, not by deference to individual trees and significant but eternally fixed views, but by a layered stacking of spaces through which a structurally-necessary aedicule-cum-lightwell rises. The higher land prices and resulting need for multi-story residences here may prefigure the time when their architecture is built as frequently in the city as in the hinterlands, as their design devices and conventions are not as dependent on raw nature as might first seem.

One reason for the success here is the wonderful job they have done in ignoring the 'keyhole' or 'cul-de-sac' suburban street planning cliché. While most of the Roche's neighbours have chosen to present their facades to this accident of unimaginative subdivision layout, this house turns from the driveway and garage which make the requisite gesture, to the rest of the house which turns to confront the best views directly. At the hub of the plan is the grand tiered stairway, the aedicule which delimits it is on a double square plan with log posts at its outer vertices. These rise most spectacularly into the master bedroom at top, a vaulted ceiling and magnificently framed window providing a heroic conclusion to the path from the street. The dialogue of curved roof-forms, especially when piled with the visible layers of different snowfalls is a wonderfully naturalistic foil to the spatial dynamism of the twisted plan and adventurous section.

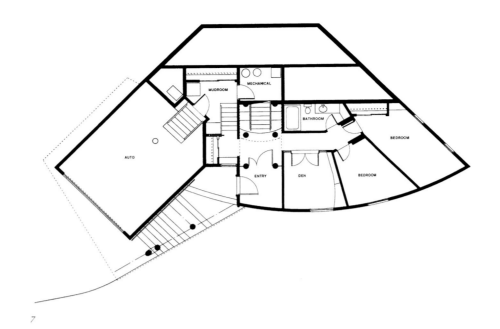

7

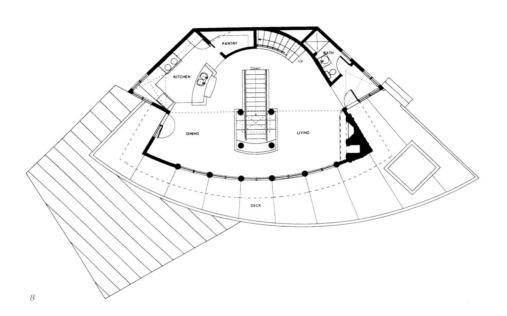

8

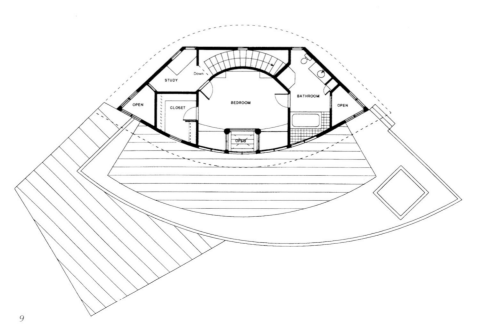

9

10

11

12

13

12   *Dining room to living room*
13&14   *Living room*

14

THOMSON HOUSE

Design 1993/Completion 1995
2,000-sq.ft. house
Hornby Island, B.C.

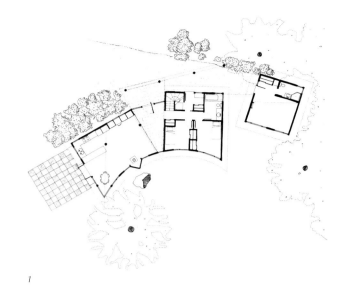

1

2

While most of our other Hornby sites are on slopes overlooking the sea, the Thomson site is relatively flat, a forest meadow with a bucolic view to meadow and farm and a partial glimpse across Little Tribune Bay. Ian and Methona Thomson have two young children, and they wanted a holiday house which would serve their growing family, with guest rooms in a separate pavilion. We thought of the house as three pavilions, a social pavilion, a sleeping pavilion and guest pavilion connected by a glass wedge-shaped atrium.

The Thomson's had camped on the site for several summers and knew where they wanted the house sited. It's placement next to the forest edge on the north side of the property allows for an outdoor terrace on the southside with maximum sun exposure. The shed roof rising towards the forest edge

that connects the two main pavilions, combined with the inverted curving facade on the view side that embraces a large maple tree are a form reminiscent of Aalto's Studio, a building we've always admired. We were quite playful with this house. The glass wedge roof that splits the main plan into two boxes pokes coyly through the curving front wall. A window that is framed by a storage wall beside the entrance forms a T for Thomson. We chose bold, saturated colours with shades of green and blue for the exterior, as well as a bright yellow that extends inside and out in the entry wedge hallway. With experience we are getting more confident with an extended palette of colours, and the darkness of the forest side demanded a more assertive range.

Continued...

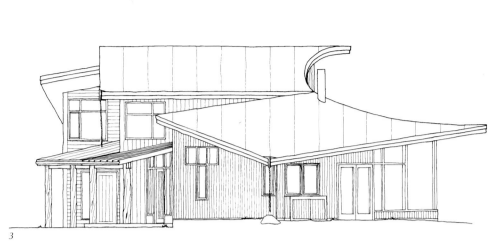

3

4

5

6

1   Main floor plan
2   Southwest elevation
3   South elevation
4   Breezeway to guesthouse
5   Northeast view
6   South elevation

Boddy

Geometrically, this is one of the most complex designs the duo has ever produced. They have set a tough geometer's problem for themselves by choosing to combine a cylinder, wedge and block. By and large the builders' problems, these choices have been solved seamlessly. In this, the Thomson house can be compared to the late domestic designs of Charles Moore, who loved to layer contradictory geometry's in plan and section, searching for the 'immaculate collisions' between them, as well as Helliwell + Smith's beloved Alvar Aalto, a direct source of some detail here and in other houses.

Considered formally, the range of forms selected by Helliwell + Smith here makes for a constantly changing variety of vistas, reveals and shadows—both inside and out, as the sun tracks around—unusually rich for a modest house of only 2,000 square feet. One of the unexpected delights of this house is the glass-covered walkway on the forest side to the left of the main entrance, a placid zone which both reconciles the sometimes overly competitive volumes, and provides a useful and visually-engaging indoor-outdoor space.

7

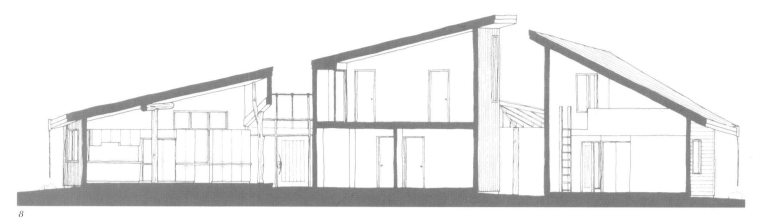

8

9

10

11

10 Kitchen
11 'Door Handle Detail' by John Grunewald
12 Entry atrium

12

HARMON HOUSE

Design 1991/Completion 1993
2,800-sq.ft. house and studio
Mayne Island, B.C.

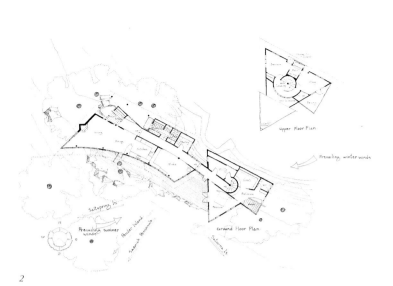

2

3

4

Even by the standards of our other houses, spectacular site conditions here determined our design. Entered uphill through a 60-acre reserve, the house is perched at the brow of two sandstone ridges, 500 feet above Navy Channel in the Gulf of Georgia, with Pender Island opposite. The site we chose with the clients is surrounded by 600-year-old craggy fir trees, some splendid, wide-branching red-barked arbutus trees, and two exposed rock ridges running parallel to the view. The curving roof profile is derived from a close analysis of the sectional profile of the brow of the hill, and is constructed of premanufactured glulam beams. The structural rhythm creates an order in the plan that is otherwise organically derived from responses to the site conditions of trees and rock ridges. View and sun coincide to the south and west, and our plan and fenestration approach attempts to also capitalize on the oblique views to the surrounding trees and rocks at a fine scale, and up and down Navy Channel at a broader one.

The owners, Greg and Isabelle Harmon approached us with very open minds. Their directive was simply for a house that spoke to and enhanced the beauty of their land. Found opportunities, such as the large sandstone slabs that appeared when blasting a road to the house, are tilted on edge at the entrance hallway and contribute to the sense that this house is an extension of the place.

Continued...

Opposite:
    Southeast elevation along sandstone ridge
2   *Site plan*
3   *Site section*
4   *View over Navy Channel with Kim Smith and Greg Harmon during early site visit*

Boddy

I first saw this house in October twilight, the oblique glass end like a boat's prow in the golden light. Later, in darkness, the same prow provided other delights, when I looked up into the fin—an octopus of internally-reflected window and mullion. Given the free flow of the rest of the house, the pure triangle of the bedroom wing seems a bit forced, a kind of false purity in a landscape of contingency. While prismatic and proud from the water side, the house has a very different dialogue with the upward thrust of the forest floor. Spectacular in every sense.

6

5

5   *Courtyard elevation*
6   *West corner of living room*
7   *Southwest terrace*
8   *View to living room with sandstone slabs*
9   *View from living room to kitchen*
10   *Weaving studio*

7

8

9

10

BROOKE–WATTS
HOUSE

Design 1989/Completion 1993
4,000-sq.ft. house
Mayne Island, B.C.

1

2

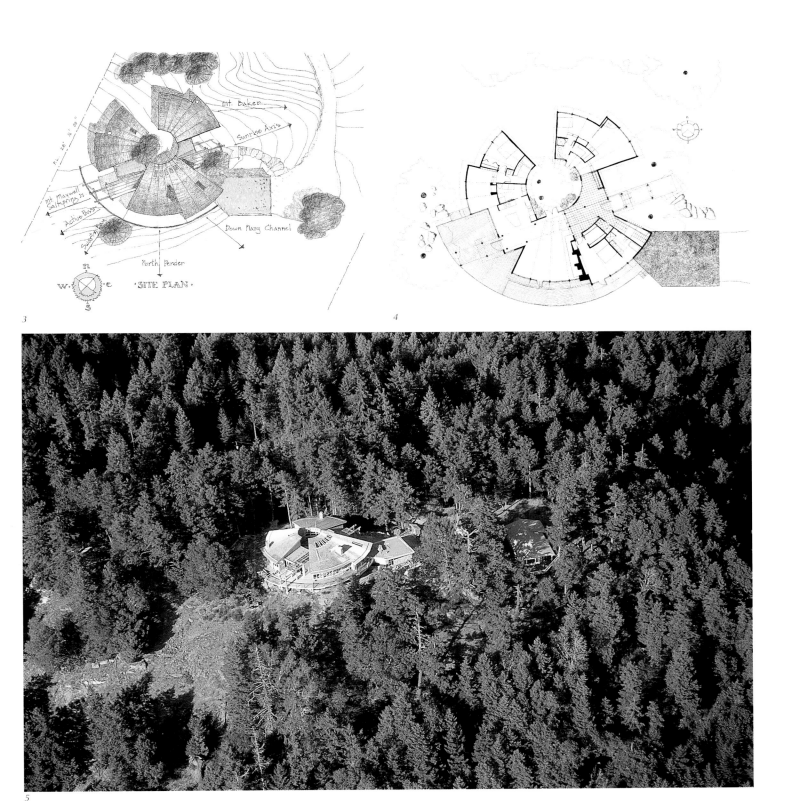

3

4

5

This house encircles the top of a hill high above Navy Channel with stunning ocean views to the south, east and west and cool forest views to the north. Dennis Watts and Cila Brooke came to us with a desire for a holiday and retirement home and an image of a limpet shell. Both are scuba divers and were intrigued with the shell image. We extended this metaphor further with the West Coast Indian 'Salish Hat' for shelter.

The crest of the hill and the metaphor of the hat suggested a radial plan. We interrupted and organized this plan with an arcade focusing on a surprise distant view. The arcade cuts through the radial geometry forming a complexity in section and organizing the plan into three pavilions of living, guest and studio wings. This is the first house where we explored a post and

Continued...

1   *Section*
2   *Perspective by Terry Brown*
3   *Site plan*
4   *Main floor plan*
5   *Aerial view*

6 *Deck arcade looking west over Satellite Channel and Saltspring Island*
7 *Arcade structure under construction*
8 *Living room*

6

7

8

beam structure that through uprights rising from main beams and connected to rafters a more varied roof form is created. Further complexity is added through the mixing of light and shadow from the linear geometry of the arcade skylights and the radial geometry of 40-foot rafters.

The house takes the 360-degree wide views of ocean and forest and frames them into more distinct and particular landscapes. An interior meditative courtyard is formed in contrast to the wide vistas presented on surrounding decks. Both intimate views of magnificent old fir trees and courtyard garden and long views to the surrounding ocean are framed by the varied aspects of the radial plan.

Boddy

With a certain ungainliness in the execution, the Brooke–Watts house sets itself a difficult formal problem by attempting to reconcile a radial plan set around a circular court (two large fir trees at the centre there first generated the design, since removed) with a boxy linear, aggressively-framed view slot, with columns and the roof truss marching from the front door through the intervening radials to pass through the other side to ocean views beyond. In this the house builds on the radial ideas of the Saks' house and the linear post and beam directionality of the Graham house, but lacks the restful quality of attendant rooms in both of those. It also lacks what Charles Moore called the 'immaculate collisions' when very different spatial orders are rammed together. This willful complexifying, the 'both-and' of very different spatial organizing devices demonstrates how far Helliwell + Smith are from conventional organic or even wood-butcher approaches, even if resulting in a kind of segmented tee-pee most evident in the perspective done by a colleague.

9

10

9   Kitchen to living room
10   Arcade looking east
11   Arcade looking west

11

GADSBY HOUSE

Design 1988/Completion 1992
2,000-sq.ft. house
Hornby Island, B.C.

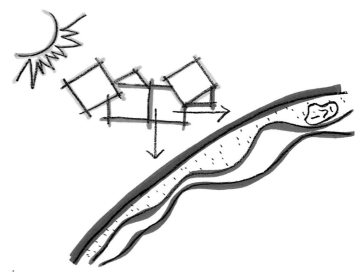

1

2

The site for this house is beside a rocky beach in a subdivision of holiday homes on Hornby Island. The north facing lots are relatively narrow and all houses are crowded by the seashore for ocean views and light. Elspeth and John Gadsby wanted an economical holiday home that they would eventually retire to. Their directive was for no curves in plan or form although they wanted their home to be ' unpredictable and hold surprise.

We sited the house angled from the shoreline rather than parallel to the ocean, so that its foreground views were up and down the rocky beach which is constantly transformed by 17-foot tides. Another advantage of this siting is that no views are towards the close neighboring houses. Capturing and balancing sunlight while exploiting the magnificent beach views to the north and east was achieved by a series of courtyards and garden rooms externally and skylights and atrium internally.

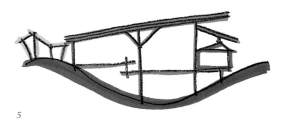

5

site plan

3

6

4

7

The structure is economically expressed with a single rising ridge beam balance on one post. The beam cuts diagonally across the main volume, again twisting the view from the obvious seascape towards the shoreline and a huge granite boulder on the foreshore. The fireplace and spiral stair help anchor the spatial dynamics and balance the sculpture. The siting of this house is organically related to site features while plan and section play more strictly with geometry.

We introduced a vibrant colour palette into this house. The strong reds, greens and yellows soak up and release light and warmth as a counterpoint to the building's cool northeast exposure.

Boddy

The Gadsby is the first house produced with Kim Smith as a full design partner. Linking back to her own student and restaurant interior work, the diagonal low zigzag forms and dynamic colour are clearly hers and welcome relief to the Blue Sky Design language which Bo Helliwell was now refining in theme and variation. Studying the plan before touring the interior and seeing the site, I have thought it a bit formalist and precious, but the diagonality of it all makes perfect sense when experienced spatially, and the scheme is clever in exploiting the hidden potentials of the site with minimal means.

8

9

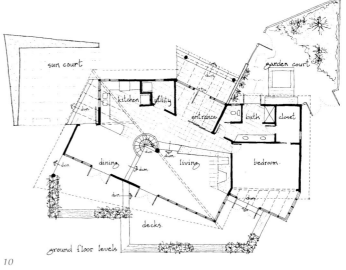

sun court

kitchen utility

garden court

entrance

bath closet

dining

living

bedroom

decks

ground floor levels

10

11

8   View to kitchen
9   Living room
10 Main floor plan
11 Entry hall and atrium

STEWART HOUSE

Design 1988/Completion 1990
1,600-sq.ft house
Hornby Island, B.C.

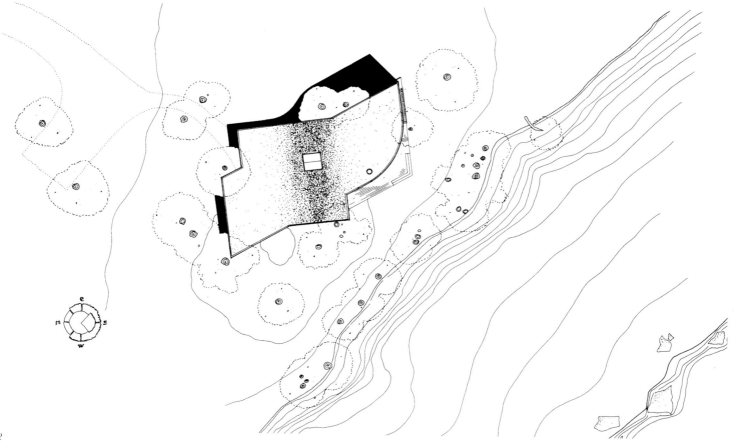

2

We first met Bill and Suzi Stewart in the summer of 1988. An engaging and enthusiastic American couple, they had fallen in love with Hornby Island and purchased a stunning piece of land high above Tribune Bay with ocean views to the south and west and forest views to the east and north. They wanted a holiday home that would suit their varied interests, from practicing Tai Chi in the forest to large gatherings of their close and extended family.

The site is sheltered from the heavy southeast winds by land mass and trees that hug the cliff edge of the property. The house is a continuation of a path through the forest towards the cliff edge and views particularly to Mount Arrowsmith on Vancouver Island. As one approaches the living room/dining room the roof rises up to embrace the tall trees of the forest, creating a space in the forest. The window wall in the main spaces is incredibly light and gives one the impression of being in an outdoor shelter. The Stewarts refer to it as an ideal form of camping.

The upstairs loft is a place for meditation. All of the finish materials chosen are natural. The Douglas fir, grey slate and yellow cedar are enduring and together they are serene. The house is a refuge in the forest; a place to reflect, to read, to meditate, to entertain, to gather family, to arrive to after long walks in the forest, a place for the drama and dreams of life. It has a wonderful quality of embrace and release, both sheltering in the forest and lifting up and out to the sea and sky.

3

Boddy

The Stewart house has one of the firm's better integration of detail and sponged wall colour, making for contemplative spaces consistent with the clients' New Age interests and practices. The spiral stair makes for a good spatial focus for the main room, the sleeping loft-cum-meditation room which it serves is placidly handsome, especially when late day winter sun reflects off the bay giving it an inner radiance. Some of the exterior details, notably the upper deck handrails demonstrate the architect's allegiance to Arts and Crafts ideals, especially as interpreted by Greene and Greene (who did a Vancouver house, sadly demolished) and Frank Lloyd Wright.

1   *Upper balcony*
2   *Site plan*
3   *South elevation*
4   *West elevation*

4

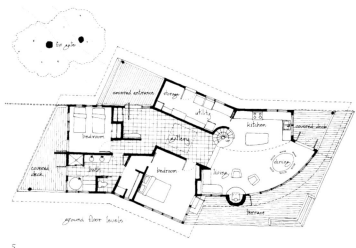

5

6

7

8

9

10

11

5   Ground floor plan
6   Main space from gallery
7   Kitchen and stair to loft
8   Section
9   Main bedroom
10 Entry gallery
11 Fireplace nook

HORNBY ISLAND AND BLUE SKY DESIGN

by Trevor Boddy

Beach driftwood, Hornby Island

While at Erickson-Massey 1968–1972, Helliwell worked with Michael McNamara, an American who had come to Vancouver to avoid the Vietnam war draft after having studied architecture at the University of Oregon. The two hit it off both as designers and as friends. Wanting a change from the pace from Vancouver, McNamara moved to Hornby Island in 1971, hoping to set up his own building firm.

By now Helliwell had worked for two of Canada's finest architects for sustained periods, with increasing responsibility from design through production of working drawings to supervision of construction. True to the romantic spirit of the times he desired a more flexible schedule, a reconnection to nature, but most of all, he wanted to learn how to build. The Northern Gulf Island of Hornby offered all of these, and Helliwell settled in himself in 1975, ultimately working there 15 years, many of them collaborating with McNamara.

Six hours and three ferries away from Vancouver, Hornby is one of the most isolated of the car-accessible Gulf Islands. Its resulting lower land prices attracted a large influx of artists, writers and refugees from the 'counter-culture' of the late 1960s and early 1970s, the previous logging-based economy having been exhausted. Hornby's attractions include wind- and water-carved beachside sandstone formations, a prodigious range of trees (notably Douglas fir, red cedar, the red-barked arbutus, and some of the northernmost flowering trees of the magnolia family) and shrubs (dogwood and wild roses everywhere announce spring in February and March), and surrounded by some of the most biologically productive waters in the world. Its natural beauty and benign climate had made it the site of Vancouver School of Art summer schools since the 1920s. Lying in the rain shadow mid-way between the mountains of Vancouver Island and the Coast Range on the mainland (Whistler is due east), Hornby has half the rain and much more sunshine than Vancouver.

All of this attracted artists Jerry Pethick, Tom Burrows, Gordon Payne and the late dean of Canadian Modern painters, Jack Shadbolt, who have all maintained studios on Hornby for the past 25 years. To these artists are added critic-curators Doris Shadbolt and Annette Hurtig, along with countless poets and craftspeople, even artistic visitors like Gordon and Marion Smith (repeat clients of Arthur Erickson, please see Smith House II on page 9), who produced this collage by ripping and reassembling a Blue Sky promotional brochure into a ruggedly nature-evoking pattern. A similar sense of playful fantasy pervades the Island, with a cooperatively-owned subdivision named after J.R.R. Tolkien's *The Shire*, and a log stackwall and driftwood community hall set with its front door a massive stump, looking like the entrance to a particularly ambitious Hobbit house.

'Blue Sky Collage' given to Kim and Bo by friend and West Vancouver artist Gordon Smith

By the early 1970s Hornby was also becoming known as a centre of innovative builders, usually called some variation of 'hippie wood-butchers' for their improvisational skill with the massive logs and plentiful driftwood found on Hornby. One of the most influential to Helliwell, McNamara, and many others is Lloyd House, whose 1970 Leaf Retreat uses a strangely twisted log as the ridge beam for a weekend summer house for a Vancouver couple still stands, as does ex-Californian wood-butcher Tim Biggins' spiral log and shake house. Both of these houses were published by Helliwell and McNamara in the 1978 Vol. 48, #7 special issue they compiled for *Architectural Design* magazine of London. I remember reading this as a second year architectural student in Calgary, the first and only Canadian content during the course of my entire studies in my favourite architectural journal. The compilation of written texts from Hornby's builders' community was as compelling to me for its text as its images, with long letters from the various wood-butchers which discussed the cooperative nature of their creations, set off by superb plan, section and analytic drawings by Helliwell and McNamara documenting the work of both Blue Sky Design and the other Hornby builders.

This *Architectural Design* issue had begun as Helliwell's history thesis while studying at London's Architectural Association Diploma School 1972–74, largely in Bernard Tschumi and Mike Gold's design studio units. After Helliwell returned to Hornby with his A.A. Diploma, he began his design and building association with McNamara. The most sophisticated of the Blue Sky designs gathered for the magazine is the Graham House for Dunlop Point on Hornby (documentation for this and the other early Blue Sky Design houses follows after this essay), with its Kahn via Erickson-inspired tartan structural grid, a rich range of post-and-beam details, and a finely orchestrated modulation of vistas, from the parking area, through gate and walkway into the house, and out towards the arbutus trees and sea beyond.

While there were very many other designs by McNamara and Helliwell singly or together on Hornby, other Gulf Islands and at Whistler, these are all extensions of the key sources for Blue Sky Design: Erickson and Massey, the Vancouver Modernists, Charles Moore and the wood-butchers. The constructions of the 1990s by Blue Sky Architecture demonstrate a quite different spatial sense and a wider range of inspiration, and are illustrated and described in the preceding portfolio section of this book. By the late 1980s Bo Helliwell had fallen in love with Kim Smith. Helliwell left Blue Sky Design in the capable hands of Michael McNamara, Tim Wyndham and team on Hornby, and by 1990 had returned to practice in Vancouver, founding a true design partnership with Kim Smith called Blue Sky Architecture, or more commonly and less confusingly, simply Helliwell + Smith.

Kim Smith maintains the house she had on Hornby before meeting Bo, and they remain active members of the still vital creative community there.

Helliwell's 1974 AA History Thesis drawing of the Leaf Retreat on Hornby Island, designed by Lloyd House

FAIRBAIRN–GLOVER HOUSE

Design 1983/Completion 1985
2,200-sq.ft. house
Hornby Island, B.C.

This is a Blue Sky Design house, designed in partnership between Bo Helliwell and Michael McNamara. The sculptural lines of the roof and a range of structural and elevation detail of this house are influential to many later Helliwell + Smith/Blue Sky Architects' houses. Julie Glover and Bruce Fairbairn purchased this meadow-like site at the end of the best sand beach on Hornby, and approached us with a number of strong ideas, both having backgrounds in urban planning (Bruce is now a rock music producer.) As well, they had a small collection of salvage building elements such as a door from a tugboat that they wanted included in the new house if possible. The graceful and symmetrical roof rises up from the meadow, with more meadow-grass planted on its roof, blending the textures of house and site.

The two flanking low roofs form both architectural and ornithological 'wings' resulting in the 'gullwing' name it is often referred to. With an atrium at the centre dividing the bedroom from social wings, interior spaces were designed to be curving, calm and embracing.

Boddy

While Helliwell + Smith have produced very few symmetrical designs, much of the repertoire of detail explored here pops up in theme and variation in their later constructions. The unity of landscape and built form is most evident here, and is more than the simple, but in this context, correct device of a grass roof. Elevations both interior and exterior are finely composed, and the softening provided by the curving roof does much to temper what could be an overpowering form. The separate studio/guest house is just as simple, with its shed forms a servant building in the best sense. A highly successful studio producer for such rock bands as Aerosmith, Styx, Bon Jovi and Van Halen, Bruce Fairbairn and his wife Julie Glover wanted a nautical theme for a quiet retreat from the noise and pace of the rock and roll business. Blue Sky have done this superbly with a wonderful synthesis of site, memory, lifestyle and dwelling.

2

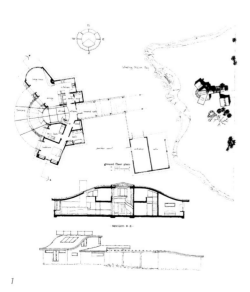

1

3

4

1 Site plan, plan, elevation, section
2 West elevation 1986
3 West elevation 1997
4 Living room
5 Terrace
6 Arcade
7 East elevation at night

5

6

7

SAKS' HOUSE

Design 1981/Completion 1982
2,200-sq.ft. house
Hornby Island, B.C.

This is an early design by Bo Helliwell, and built by Tim Wyndham and Bo with Blue Sky Design and its extended ensemble of talented Hornby craftsmen, and filled with a fine collection of the work of Hornby craft and fine artists. Jim and Judy Saks of Cleveland purchased this site half way up the slopes of Hornby's Mt Geoffrey, with panoramic views west and north to Vancouver Island and Georgia Strait. Like so many later Helliwell + Smith's, this was a recreation home for extended summer stays for them and their family, to be used later as a retirement home.

The basic spiral conception was a response to the land form of the hill. The two focal points of the spiral are the earth-bound stone mass of the fireplace anchored into the hillside and the skyward-bound spiral staircase ascending to the lookout tower. Heavy and light play off each other—it's a house of contrasting elements

spiraling inward to the fire and outward over the trees. This synthesis of organic form and rigorous structure permits a variety of textural, light and spatial experiences inside. The design was conceived on a mere two sheets of 1/8" scale drawings. The finer details were improvised and refined during the collaborative building process.

Boddy

This house is an early *tour-de-force* by Helliwell and team, demonstrating his mastery of the spiral building lessons provided both by his former employer Etienne Gaboury, and to a lesser extent Tim Biggins and other Hornby wood-butcher experiments. Viewed from below on this steep mountain slope, the house provides a delightful response to landscape, and more than mere mimesis, but a kind of nature retooled.

1

2

1   Structural frame
2   Northwest elevation
3   Plan and elevation

The guest wing, separated from the main spiral house by a breezeway, has a rich range of eminently inhabitable spaces. This house is notable for the increasing sophistication of its detailing, and the rich array of spaces as it rises in section to an eagle eerie-like meditation chamber above the bedroom, these very birds often visible outside. The quality of craftsmanship by this all-Hornby team is excellent throughout, but with special accolades to John Grunewald for his built-in stairway and custom furniture. As no other British Columbia house of the 1980s, the Saks' house demonstrates a Ruskinian sensibility and Arts and Crafts' techniques thriving in the special conditions of Hornby Island.

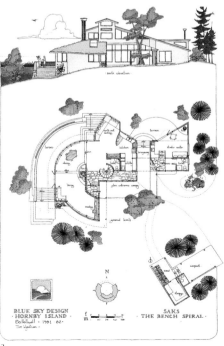

3

4

4   Spiral stair
5   Entry hall
6   Dining room
7   Living room

5

6

7

GRAHAM HOUSE

Design 1976/Completion 1983
6,700-sq.ft. house
Hornby Island, B.C.

This house was both the first design collaboration between Bo Helliwell and Michael McNamara and still the largest house either has done. As such, it was an excellent laboratory for developing both design and building skills. A rationally linear plan derived from their exposure to Erickson was embellished with a more organic range of details by the Blue Sky team that built the house. The house intentionally withdraws behind an ancient Indian mound, leaving a broad lawn and highly individualistic arbutus and fir trees to be part of the seascape, and to protect the house from the extreme southeasterly storms which buffet the point upon which it sits. This siting also had the effect of reducing the perceived volume of this large house, guest and swimming pool pavilions. These were built in stages over many years around a sunny, wind-screened courtyard.

Many lessons from this house, including sensitively unorthodox siting, internally-expressed structure, and organically integrated detail have carried on into the formerly quite different work of Helliwell + Smith.

Boddy

Like Frank Lloyd Wright, Arthur Erickson's imitators produce worse and worse houses the closer they get to directly imitating the master. This is one of the handful of the best Ericksonian houses produced in the 1970s in the wake of the innovations of the Smith and Graham houses, likely because both designers left Erickson's employ before blinding themselves to other sources of inspiration. The canopied entrance axis from gate, past bathing pavilion and guest houses to the main house itself is in a word, spectacular, amplified after passing through the massive door to turn past bold post and beam and fireplace details to revel in the 180-degree range of ocean and view, the rocks and saved trees giving the whole ensemble a Japanese villa quality. The Grahams still live here nearly 20 years after first commissioning the design, high praise for a rigorous and powerfully-conceived Modern house.

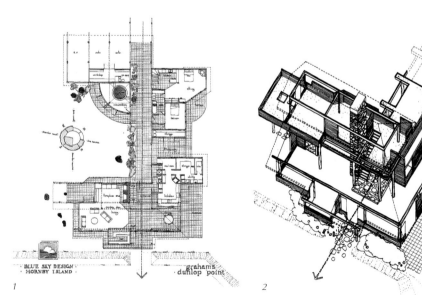

1   2

3

1 Floor plan
2 Axonometric
3 Dunlop Point
4 Post and beam/light detail
5 Living room

COHEN HOUSE

Design 1997–1998
4,000-sq.ft. house
West Vancouver, B.C.

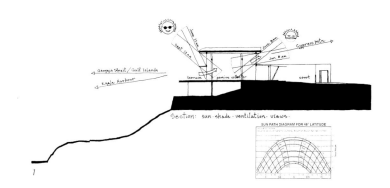

1

This house learns both from the Harvey House, with a simplicity in plan and section and from the more complex Greenwood House, with an organic rather than geometric relationship of plan to site.

The site is an irregular shaped and steeply sloping lot in a subdivision of West Vancouver. The building bridges over a natural gully formed by two granite outcrops while creating a platform with dramatic and sweeping views of Georgia Straight. The curving southwestern wall responds to these views and creates a dynamic series of spaces, views, and light conditions. The gently arched roof nestles the house in the landscape and provides high vaulted volumes in the main living spaces and a two-story bedroom area on the north side. The upper floor opens out to a natural rock outcrop to the east and the landscaped roof of the garage, which slips into a cleft in the rocks below. The natural rock terrain and existing vegetation of fir, cedar, arbutus and pine trees as well as salel and mountain ash will be retained as much as possible throughout the site. A more formal landscape will be contained in the entrance courtyard.

Boddy

This unbuilt house is a useful foil to explore the graphic house style and model techniques of Helliwell + Smith. Given how important topography is to virtually all their house designs the representation of slopes is crucial, seen in the *poché* of the elevations, while the silhouette schematic perspective is a particularly useful means of representing a house on mountainous terrain, the picturesque aesthetic captured in only a few lines. Early design work for their houses almost always starts with gestural moves in response to landscape contingencies tested in plan and section conventionally, builder's knowledge of structure and framing implicitly sizing rooms. Models are more of a design development tool, a tectonic test on a topographic base.

2

1 *Conceptual drawing*
2–4 *Models*
5 *Conceptual drawing*

3

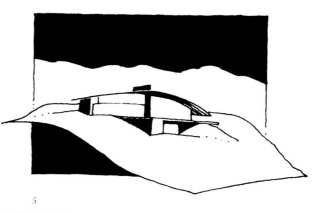

4

5

DRYVYNSYDE HOUSE

Design 1997–1999
2,700-sq.ft. house
Galiano Island, B.C.

The Vancouver clients had long kept a vacation cabin on this site, and asked us to replace it with a much larger retirement house on the same location. This house sits on a peninsula formed by a jutting series of sandstone shelves, each shaped into similar forms. We took the angles and shapes from the site's geological feature to form the walls and shed roofs of the four pavilions of this house, each lifted in a different direction, but connecting together to form the sheltered, southwest-facing garden courtyard the clients mandated. The differential lifts of the four pavilions allow for clerestory lighting for key living spaces, while exterior window-walls orient to the north and Gossip Island and east to Active Pass, the distant volcanic cone of Mt. Baker visible to the southeast. Materials are natural, with slate and alder wood floors, exposed fir building structure, and horizontal exterior siding. The roofs are metal with a grey patina surface.

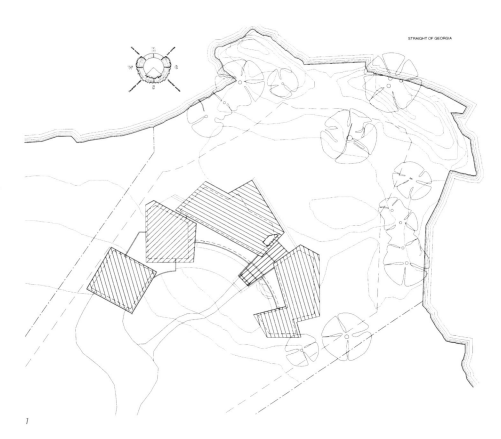

STRAIGHT OF GEORGIA

1

1   Site plan
2   Northeast elevation
3   Plan
4   Southwest elevation

Boddy

I was with Helliwell + Smith on their first site visit before design started for the Dryvynsyde house. They carted their own survey transit and were soon recording data, both to ensure the accurate location of trees, rocks and the other important natural features which so often drive their designs, but also as a way to walk the site in non-intuitive ways, thereby discovering hidden qualities. Walking the site is one of the most important and under-rated of all architectural skills, and they are masters of this combination of sight, touch, smell and listening, and it was a marvel to watch them pace and measure, the random runs of their golden retriever Charlie providing comic relief. Kim noted then sketched the sandstone formation, and these were brought back to West Vancouver after an idyllic June afternoon, forming the organizing idea of their design. While given gently from the site, this is also creative invention of the purest sort.

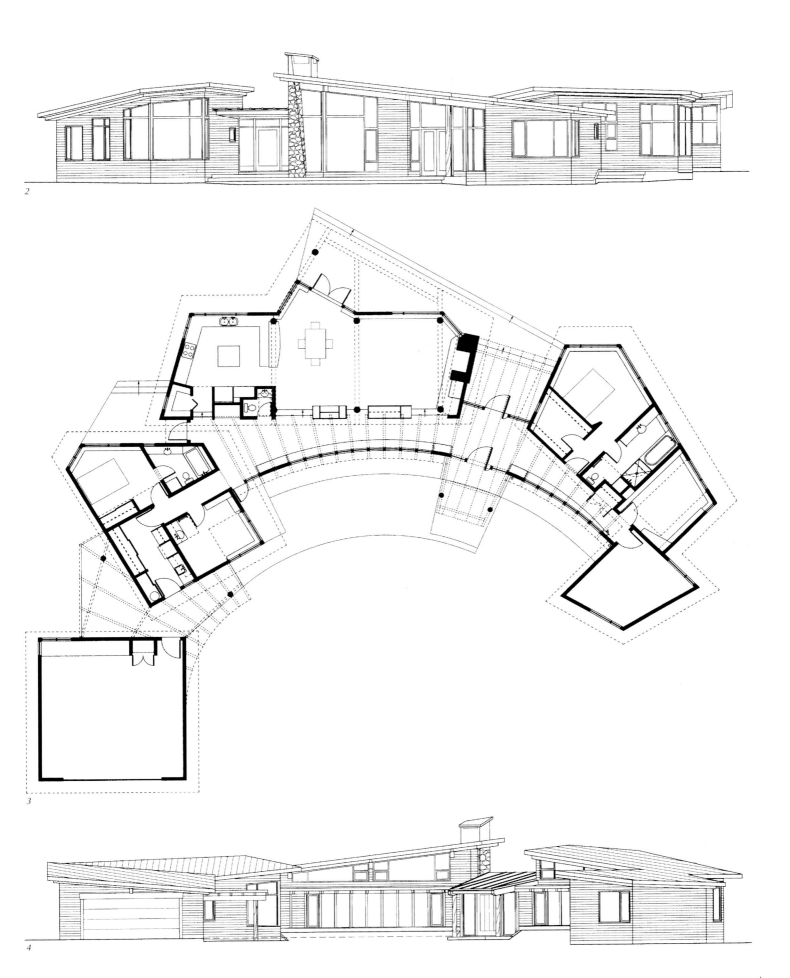

2

3

4

Kim Smith

Kim Smith was born in Kingston, Canada in 1953. She received a degree in film and English from Queen's University in 1976. Kim then worked in reforestation planting trees for five years. During this period she also built a 40-foot catamaran and sailed it from Lake Ontario to the Caribbean. In 1980 she entered the University of British Columbia School of Architecture, graduating in 1984.

During the mid-80s she worked on pavilion design for EXPO 86, furthered her architectural studies at the Pratt Institute in New York and the Architectural Association in London and travelled extensively in Europe, Asia and Africa. Kim began working with Blue Sky Design, on Hornby Island in 1987 and in 1989 moved to West Vancouver to lay the foundation for Blue Sky Architecture with Bo Helliwell.

Kim has been a design critic and thesis advisor at the UBC School of Architecture and has lectured and exhibited internationally. She is a member of the Vancouver League for Studies in Architecture and the Environment, sits on several Design Review Panels and continues to collect art, sail, and ski avidly.

Bo Helliwell

Bo Helliwell was born in Thunder Bay, Canada, in 1944. He received a degree in Environmental Studies from the University of Manitoba in 1969 and graduated in 1977 from the Architectural Association, London. In Winnipeg, he worked with Etienne Gaboury from 1965 to 1968 and in Vancouver, from 1968 to 1972, with Arthur Erickson and Geoff Massey. During this period of time he was also a member of the Whistler Mountain Ski Patrol. An epic overland travel from Europe, across Asia in 1974 helped change his direction from urban to rural and he settled on Hornby Island to become a designer-builder and a founder of Blue Sky Architecture in 1975.

In 1984, Blue Sky was invited to exhibit and speak at Berlin's International Exposition (IBA) and many more exhibitions and speaking tours followed. In 1989, an invitation by the Vancouver League to exhibit in Vancouver helped shift the focus from Hornby Island to the city and Bo and Kim Smith moved to West Vancouver, formalized their architectural credentials and established Blue Sky Architecture.

Bo has been a design critic and thesis advisor at the UBC School of Architecture and has lectured and exhibited internationally. He is a member of the Vancouver League for Studies in Architecture and the Environment and is a past Council Member of the Architectural Institute of British Columbia. Mountain and sea adventures remain a passion.

List of Credits

Helliwell + Smith•Blue Sky Architecture

Architects
Bo Helliwell MAIBC RAIC
Kim Smith MAIBC RAIC
Bruce Ramsay
Andrew Best
Kristina Leaning
Rafael Gomez Moriana
Richard Peck
Robert Tyndal

Builders
Neil Corbett
Alan Fletcher
John Grunewald
Glen Lynskey
Peter Nichol
Steve Peters
Ray Stanley
Tim Wyndham

Blue Sky Design

Designers
Bo Helliwell
Michael McNamara

Builders
Ed Colin
Steve Peters
Tim Wyndham

Helliwell + Smith • Blue Sky Architecture

October 1998

Canadian Wood Design Awards Exhibition

Architectural Center, Vancouver B.C.

1998

Canadian Wood Council Design Honour Award

The Bridge House, Denman Island B.C.

1998

Canadian Wood Council Island Design Merit Award

Fishbones, the Greenwood House, Galiano B.C.

1998

Lieutenant Governor's Merit Award, AIBC

The Bridge House, Denman Island B.C.

1997

Best in the West Honour Award, Western Living Magazine

Fishbones, the Greenwood House, Galiano Island B.C.

June 22–August 20, 1995

The Architect's Dwelling: A Self-Portrait

Design Exchange, Toronto, Ontario

An exhibition by Maison d'Etre showcasing 29 Canadian Architects and their homes

April 19-23, 1995

75 Years of Residential Design in British Columbia

Selected exhibition of the best of residential design in British Columbia over the past 75 years

The Architectural Institute of British Columbia, Vancouver B.C.

April 15-May 15, 1995

Touch the Earth Lightly, Simon Fraser Downtown Campus

Selected Exhibition of Environmentally Responsive Design in British Columbia in conjunction with 75th anniversary of Architectural Institute of British Columbia, Vancouver B.C.

June 1–June 30, 1993

Women In Architecture

Exhibition of seven recent works as part of a 'Group Show' of 30 women in architecture

The Landing, Vancouver B.C.

April 1-April 30,1993

Residential Design in B.C. 'Group Show' of 30 B.C. Architects

Exhibition of one recent house as part of a 'Group Show' of 30 B.C. architects

Architectural Institute of British Columbia, Vancouver B.C.

Blue Sky Design

October 10-27, 1989

Blue Sky Design, Hornby Island and Beyond

Exhibition and illustrated lecture for The Vancouver League for Studies in Architecture and the Environment

Simon Fraser Downtown Campus, Vancouver, B.C.

June 1987

A House for Today, Architectural Design

Exhibition of Prize Winners for International Competition at The Royal Institute of British Architects, London, England and other galleries throughout Great Britain

February 3-19, 1987

Island Immersion

Island Immersion, the Art and Architecture of Hornby Island' (including a lecture on the architecture of Hornby Island)

North Park Gallery, Victoria B.C.

1986

Institute of Architects exhibition of Hornby Island architecture

Kiel, West Germany

March 1986

Museum of Architecture

Exhibition on the architecture of Hornby Island

Warsaw, Poland

March 1986

Technical University exhibition of Hornby Island architecture

Warsaw, Poland

February 1986

Constructa International Exposition Institute of Architects

Hannover, West Germany

January 1986

International Exhibition, exhibition of Hornby Island architecture

Hamburg, West Germany

September–October 1985

Bouwcentrum 'Huis In Eigen Hand' (House by your own Hand)

Exhibition and symposium with illustrated lectures, sponsored by the city of Rotterdam and the Berlin senate

Rotterdam, Holland

April 1985

Palazzo Taverna

Exhibition of Hornby Island architecture sponsored by The Italian Institute of Architecture and by the Goethe Institute

Rome, Italy

October 1984

Berlinische Gallery "Kooperatives Bauen" (Cooperative Building)

Exhibition of Hornby Island architecture, in conjunction with the IBA, in Berlin

May 1981

Robson Square Media Center

Exhibition of Hornby Island architecture, in conjunction with the Circle Craft

Vancouver, B.C.

March 1981

Brakendale Art Gallery

Exhibition of Hornby Island architecture and associated arts and crafts, together with a regional building symposium

Brakendale, B.C.

BIBLIOGRAPHY

HELLIWELL + SMITH/BLUE SKY ARCHITECTURE PUBLICATIONS

1998 Wood Design Awards. (no. 23, Fall 1998). Janam Publications Inc. for the Canada Wood Council, Ottawa, Ontario, pp. 18–19 (Bridge House Honour Award), 24–25 (Fishbones Merit Award).

"Blue Sky Build on West Coast Design." *North Shore Now* (North Vancouver, April 1993).

Boddy, Trevor. "Fish House on a Hot Stone Plate." *Globe and Mail* (Toronto, December 20, 1997).

Boddy, Trevor. "The Sorensen House, Hornby Island." *The National Post* (Toronto, January 23, 1999).

Cruckshank, Tom. "Fish Story." *Harrowsmith Country Life* (Montreal, vol. XXIII, no. 145, April 1998).

Davey, Peter. "Natural Forces." *Architectural Review* (London, vol. CCI, no. 1199, January 1997), pp 60–63.

Drohan, Joyce. "Women's Work." *The Canadian Architect* (Toronto, vol. 38, no. 11, November 1993), pp. 24–25.

"Fishbones House, Galiano Island, B.C." *Arcade* (Seattle, vol. XV, no. 2, Winter 1996), cover, pp. 24–27.

Haden, Bruce. "Bone Structure." *The Canadian Architect* (Toronto, vol. 43, no. 7, July 1998), pp 17–19.

Helliwell, Bo & Kim Smith. "Design for the Gulf Islands." *Gulf Islands Guardian* (Gulf Islands, vol. 5, no. 2, Fall 1995), pp. 9–11.

Leidl, David. "A Man's Cottage is his Castle." *B.C. Business* (Toronto, vol. 25, no. 9, September 1997), pp. 50–60.

MacLellan, Lila. "Best in the West." *Western Living* (Vancouver, vol. 22, no. 10, December 1997), pp. 30–42.

McPhedran, Kerry. "Gull Wing House on Hornby Island." *City and Country Home* (Toronto, vol. 12, no. 3, June/July 1993), pp. 34–40.

McPherson, Kerry. "Look What They've Done to My Neighbourhood." *Vancouver Magazine* (Vancouver, vol. 24, no. 11, November 1991), pp. 44–54.

Robb, Dianne. "Hornby Homes." *About the House* (British Columbia, February 1994), pp. 17–19.

Sorenson, Jean. "Architectural Excellence Organic Architecture West Coast Style." *Homes & Cottages* (Toronto, vol. 5, no. 5, Fall 1995), pp. 60–65.

"Spatial Designs that Liven Up Every Aspect of Your Home." *Our House* (Osaka, vol. 92, Spring 1991), pp. 10–28.

Wood Calendar 1997. Council of Forest Industries, Ottawa, Canada. (Fishbones House)

BLUE SKY DESIGN PUBLICATIONS

"A House for Today." *Architectural Design* (London, vol. 56, 1986), p. 25. (Major international ideas competition; Bo Helliwell commended)

"Astragal." *The Architects Journal* (vol. 184, no. 30, July 1986), p. 17.

Backhouse, Fran. "Grass Roots Roofing." *Harrowsmith Magazine* (Camden East, vol. XII, no. 77, January/February 1988), pp. 69–77.

Blomeyer, Gerald. "Savage Dreams." *Architectural Review* (London, vol. CLXXXIII, no. 1092, February 1988), pp. 27–33.

Blomeyer, Gerald & Barbara Tietze. *La Casa E' Come Un Albero.* Rome, Italy: Edizioni Lavoro, 1985, pp. 70–75.

Blomeyer, Gerald & Barbara Tietze. "Learning by Building." In *Die Andere Bauarbeit* (Alternative Building). Stuttgart, Germany: Deutsche Verlags-Anstalt, 1984, pp. 54–59.

Dom (Warsaw, no. 23, March 1986). (Report on the Hornby exhibition)

Freeman, Robert. "Lifestreams 'Home as a Fantasy'." *Comox District Free Press* (Courtenay, February 6, 1987).

Godley, Elizabeth. "The Rise of 'Counter-culture' Houses." *The Vancouver Sun* (Vancouver, October 14, 1989).

"Graham Residence." *Housing Review* (Japan, no. 12, 1985), pp. 66–68.

Grunewald, John. "Building a Cantilevered Tread Spiral Stair." *Fine Homebuilding* (Newtown, USA, no. 35, October/November 1986), pp. 74–79.

"Hand Crafted Every Step of the Way." *House Beautiful's Building* (Manual, USA, Fall/Winter 1983–1984), pp. 74–77.

Helliwell, Bo. "The Bench Spiral." *Fine Homebuilding* (Newtown, USA, no. 35, October/November 1986), pp. 74–79.

Helliwell, Bo. "The Bench Spiral." *Wood World* (Vancouver, vol.11, no.2, 1983), pp. 6–8.

Helliwell, Bo & Michael McNamara. "A Hand Built House on Hornby Island." *Wood World* (Vancouver, vol. 8, No 4, 1981), pp. 2–5.

Helliwell, Bo & Michael McNamara. "Handbuilt Hornby." *Architectural Design*, (London, vol. 48, no.7, 1978), pp. 443–491.

Jencks, Charles & William Chaitkin. *Architecture Today.* England: Abrams, 1982, pp. 225–259.

McPhedran, Kerry. "Hornby Island's Eagle House." *City and Country Homes* (Toronto, vol. 11, no. 4, May 1992), pp. 54–66.

Mitchell, Harris. "Island Beauty." *Canadian Homes* (Toronto, July 1978).

Ovenell-Carter, Julie. "At Home With Bruce Fairbairn." *Western Living* (Vancouver, vol. 17, no. 10, September 1987), pp. 34–45.

"Sorensen Residence." *Housing Review* (Japan, no. 11, 1985), pp. 58–61.

"True to Form." *Canadian Interiors* (Toronto, vol. 23, no. 3, March 1986).

Wood, Daniel. "In Search of Canadian Design." *Select Homes* (Toronto, August 1986), pp. 18–19.

ACKNOWLEDGMENTS

Bo Helliwell and Kim Smith would like to acknowledge the support of their families, particularly Mary and Phoebe, their coworkers, especially Bruce Ramsay and Richard Peck, their clients who are part of the triad that produces these works and the builders and craftspeople who are the other essential part of good architecture and building. We would also like to thank Peter Davey for his kind Preface and support.

PHOTOGRAPHY CREDITS

Trevor Boddy 82 (1)

Custom Colour 56 (2,3), 72 (2), 73 (3), 86 (bottom), 91 (3), 94 (1,2)

Greg Eymundson Insight 42—43, 46 (19,20), 47 (21)

Alan Fletcher back cover, 22 (15)

John Fulker 11 (right), 21 (10, 11), 24, 25, 26 (18—20), 27 (21, 22, 23), 28 (2) 30 (6,7), 31 (8), 32, 36, 37, 39 (2,3), 41 (10, 44 (15—18), 48 (2), 49 (4), 50 (5), 51 (7), 52 (8), 53 (10), 54 (11), 55 (12), 57 (4), 59 (11), 60 (12,13), 61 (14), 62 (2), 63 (5), 64 (8), 67 (12), 68, 70 (5—7), 71 (8,10), 74 (6,8), 76 (9,10), 77 (11), 79 (4,6,7), 80 (9, opposite, 11), 83 (3,4), 84 (6,7), 85 (9,11), 88 (2), 89 (5), 90 (2), 92 (5), 93 (7), 94 (3), 95 (4,5)

Gaboury archives 11

Bo Helliwell 9, 10, 18 (6), 21 (12), 22 (13, 14), 28 (1), 39 (7), 55 (13), 56 (1), 57 (5,6), 59 (10), 69 (4), 73 (5), 74 (7), 86 (top), 90 (1), 96 (2,3), 97 (4)

Michael McNamara 89 (4)

Patrizia Menton 35 (12—15), 47 (22), 63 (4,6), 65 (9), 66 (10), 67 (11), 85 (10)

Peter Powles front cover, 17 (4), 23, 89 (6), 92 (4), 93 (6)

Leanna Rathkelly 39 (6), 42 (11,12), 48 (1)

Simon Scott 78 (2)

Oscar Sieg 88 (3), 89 (7)

Kim Smith 5, 14, 16 (3), 20 (9), 29 (3), 71 (9)

INDEX

Bold page numbers refer to featured projects